Silence Kills

PRAISE FOR *SILENCE KILLS*

"*Silence Kills* is a love letter to creating significant conversations and authentic influence in how we communicate. Author Scott Harvey captures the power of words in a fun and unique way that made *Silence Kills* readable, dynamic, and also prescriptive. Scott's specialized law enforcement background, training, and storytelling creates a roadmap to authentic connection and legacy that lasts."

—**Clint Pulver,** Speaker and Author of *I Love it Here*

"Not all professional speakers are good writers, and not all writers can handle themselves on stage. With *Silence Kills*, Scott has proven himself in both areas. Reading *Silence Kills* feels like being a part of Scott's audience at a live event. I highly recommend it!"

—**Grant Baldwin,** Author and Founder of *The Speaker Lab*

"*Silence Kills* is a MUST READ for anyone interested in taking their communication skills to the Next Level!"

—**Cliff Ravenscraft,** Host of *The Cliff Ravenscraft Show* and *The Mindset Answer Man*

"When Scott taught the concepts in *Silence Kills* to our leadership team, it helped our company streamline our communication process. Scott's storytelling is second to none. We will be purchasing copies of *Silence Kills* for our whole team. I highly recommend you do the same."

—Amy Wilkins, President and CEO,
Marine Solutions, INC.

"Most books about communication are either too simplistic or too convoluted to help individuals or teams move the needle towards effective communication. Scott Harvey's book *Silence Kills* is neither of these. The concrete strategies in *Silence Kills* are the WD-40 that you need to reduce friction and increase effectiveness at all levels of your organization. Bonus points? They work in every aspect of your personal life, too."

—Diana Alt, Executive Coach and
Career Growth Strategist

"In leading an organization that is spread out across the country, it is critical for us to have good communication. Scott does a masterful job of using his experience in law enforcement to emphasize the critical nature of speaking up. A great reminder of what happens when we don't speak up and people naturally fill in the blanks with their own conclusions. Highly Recommended!"

—Ked Frank, Founder and President, Refuge for Women

"Wow! *Silence Kills* just moved into my top book recommendations for my coaching clients and friends! Every page kept pulling me to the next! Scott is a masterful storyteller who writes with heart, humor, and a bias toward real application that is absolutely refreshing! I laughed out loud frequently, I teared up 3 times, learned practical tools to break the silence, and feel massively equipped to do better! Do yourself a favor and read *Silence Kills* now!"

—**Mark Keene,** Author and Owner,
Transformation Coaching

"Scott is a genius when it comes to communication! *Silence Kills* is THE toolkit needed for solving the biggest communication challenges faced by leaders and organizations today—nothing will be left to chance. Read *Silence Kills*!"

—**James Hilliard,** CEO Hilliard International Group

"*Silence Kills* is a must read for business leaders and humans in general! Scott's approach to communication is concise and easy to apply on and off the clock. Highly recommend!"

—**Kimberly Schilling,** Owner, Creative Works

SILENCE KILLS

Communication Tactics
to Speak with Confidence
and Build Your Influence

SCOTT HARVEY

Hostage Negotiator & Business Communication Coach

NEW YORK

LONDON • NASHVILLE • MELBOURNE • VANCOUVER

Silence Kills

Communication Tactics to Speak with Confidence and Build Your Influence

Published in New York, New York, by Morgan James Publishing. Morgan James is a trademark of Morgan James, LLC. www.MorganJamesPublishing.com

Proudly distributed by Ingram Publisher Services.

A **FREE** ebook edition is available for you
or a friend with the purchase of this print book.

CLEARLY SIGN YOUR NAME ABOVE

Instructions to claim your free ebook edition:
1. Visit MorganJamesBOGO.com
2. Sign your name CLEARLY in the space above
3. Complete the form and submit a photo
   of this entire page
4. You or your friend can download the ebook
   to your preferred device

ISBN 9781636980157 paperback
ISBN 9781636980164 ebook
Library of Congress Control Number:
2022941952

Cover & Interior Design by:
Christopher Kirk
www.GFSstudio.com

Morgan James is a proud partner of Habitat for Humanity Peninsula
and Greater Williamsburg. Partners in building since 2006.

Get involved today! Visit MorganJamesPublishing.com/giving-back

TABLE OF CONTENTS

INTRODUCTION

"**A**LL CLEAR! Shooter is in custody." I breathed a sigh of relief as the SWAT commander called across the radio. When the officers finally made entry into the house, they found containers of ammunition staged in the middle of every room and guns squirreled away like some deranged chipmunk storing nuts for the winter. These weapons were ready for him to quickly grab in any room.

Hours earlier, when the original call came in to dispatch, all we knew was that rounds had been fired from inside the house, penetrating the walls of the next-door neighbors. Shortly after, the SWAT team was en route, including the hostage negotiator. Me.

The SWAT team set a perimeter to keep the suspect from escaping. While they evacuated the neighbors, I started calling the suspect's phone. My job, amidst the chaos, was to get him talking. When he picked up the phone, the negotiations started the way they always did. He cussed me and hung up. I called back. He threatened me and hung up. I called back. He threatened my family and hung up. I called back. Eventually, he quit hanging up. I wanted to help him, and it was my job to convince him of this fact. Rapport HAD to be established. That was my main job from the outset.

After HOURS of asking the right questions, actively listening to his answers—without judgment—as he vented his frustrations and fears, and building rapport, I finally convinced him that surrendering peacefully was the way he maintained control here. It was the smart move. It was the BEST way this could work out for him. I talked him through the entire process so that he knew exactly what to expect from the SWAT team when they met him in the driveway. Thanks to our professional SWAT team, he was taken into custody exactly the way they told me they would do it.

After he was cuffed, checked for weapons, and the house cleared by the SWAT team to make sure no one else was in there, I met with him in the street face-to-face—just like I told him we would do. I am a man of my word.

I was still riding my adrenaline high, but I think he may have been dealing with MUCH more adrenaline than I was.

He thanked me for listening to him. The team loaded him into a patrol car, and then he was taken for a mental health evaluation.

All in all, it was a good day.

Everyone walked away from the scene. The only shots fired went off before we arrived on the scene, shot by the man we now had in custody. And, thankfully, no one was injured. There's no doubt this situation had the potential to be a TERRIBLE day for our community.

It begs the question: How does someone armed with a simple telephone take an individual they have never met—a stranger who barricaded himself in his own house stockpiled with weapons and ammunition for a real-life shootout at the O.K. Corral—and talk him into leaving those weapons behind and walking out without another round fired by either him or the police?

In one word: TRAINING.

In my twenty years of law enforcement, the one constant was training. Whether it was for a basic traffic stop or my role as an FBI-trained hostage negotiator, we trained for EVERYTHING. Every year, I received training in:

- Hostage Negotiation
- Media and Public Relations
- Drug Abuse Resistance Education (D.A.R.E.) Youth Education at both the state and international levels
- Firearms safety and practice (at least three, eight-hour range days throughout the year)
- CPR/First Aid
- Defensive Tactics
- Honor Guard

And all this is on TOP of the 40 hours of state required in-service training. We spent hours and days training in each area every year. Some areas every month.

We trained. All. The. Time.

I was talking with an orthopedic surgeon friend of mine recently and discovered that Kentucky law enforcement officers are required to do more in-service training hours each year than surgeons. I don't know how I feel about this when it comes to surgery, but it sure makes me respect the men and women who pin a badge on every day to go to work.

I guess the biggest difference between our training and that of a surgeon is that we trained in skills we hoped we never had to use. I never had to fire my gun in the line of duty, thank God. But every time I was at the range, my mind prepared so that IF that time ever came, I wouldn't hesitate. I would do what I had been trained to do. That doesn't mean we turned off our brains, because any lethal force situation requires precise decision-making. Hesitation can get you killed. Our number one job was to protect the public.

So we trained.

Honor Guard training was no different. Honor Guard was one of the jobs that I took very seriously. This is a specialized unit that you have probably seen before; you just didn't realize what you were seeing. If you have witnessed police, fire, EMS, or military personnel carrying flags in parades or posting the flags at graduations, you have seen an Honor Guard in action. Their uniform is usually quite different from what the rank and file personnel wear, and they perform VERY precise movements that render special honor to each ceremony or event.

Our Honor Guard participated in parades, at graduations, and traveled the country helping with Line of Duty funerals. We trained every month for hours at a time.

Like most law enforcement training, we spent most of our time preparing for the worst-case scenario.

We hadn't had a Line of Duty death at my agency since 1941, but we trained anyway. Because, God forbid, if we had a

Line of Duty death, we'd only have three to five days to pull off a precisely choreographed event attended by THOUSANDS of people from all over the country.

When we assisted other agencies with their Line of Duty funerals, we often worked with hundreds of other Honor Guard members from around the country. Sometimes we were tasked with casket guard detail—at least one Honor Guard member stands at a modified attention next to the casket of the fallen officer at all times so that they are never alone. But the most important tasks at these funerals are always reserved for the host agency. They served as pallbearers, worked closely with the family, and folded the flag that draped the casket at the graveside—as comrades of the fallen officer, this honor was theirs to perform.

I can't tell you how many times we practiced flag folding over an empty casket at our local funeral home—just in case something ever happened to one of our own. Keep in mind that a properly-folded American flag shows ONLY blue with stars. There should be NO red or white stripes showing at all when folded correctly.

As I mentioned earlier, the folding of the flag is done graveside by the host Honor Guard and then presented to the family of the fallen officer. These flags end up being put into cases and displayed by the family for GENERATIONS as a way of honoring the ultimate sacrifice that was made by their loved one.

We were VERY aware of the fact that we had ONE chance to get this right in front of thousands of people at a STRESS-FUL event. So we practiced this. A LOT.

YOUR CRISIS IS COMING

A crisis is coming that you will be forced to deal with.

- Your product harms a customer.
- An employee scandal erupts.
- Board members are upset.

You will have a choice: stay silent and watch the emergency unfold, hoping there aren't too many casualties. Or communicate clearly to negotiate a positive outcome.

Proper training will get you through ANY situation—muscle memory is a real thing. But training needs to be done strategically and regularly. Because when the stress is high enough, our brain is less efficient. Thoughts are harder to form. We either freeze, or training takes over—setting into motion whatever we planned and practiced ahead of time.

This book is your training. After reading it:

- You won't be afraid of saying the wrong thing.
- You will know what you can say.
- You will know the best tactics to deliver your message.
- Your clients and customers will trust you.
- You will lead your team with confidence.

There will be a crisis. You will be able to handle it—or better yet, AVOID it—because you have read this book and practiced the principles.

Now, training isn't always fun, but if you have ever hung out with a bunch of cops, you know that we can find a way to have fun in ANY situation.

Pro Tip: Do NOT sit next to a police officer at a quiet event. There's a good chance they will get you laughing at the WORST possible time while they maintain an impressive poker face.

While this book is serious training, we will have some fun along the way. I don't know any other way to train. The difference being, most of my law enforcement training was to sharpen skills I hoped I never needed. I just couldn't afford to have them perish from non-use.

The tactics in this book will be skills you will use EVERY day. And if you do, they will not only make you better at work— they will make you a better spouse, a better parent, and a better friend. You will be the one that people count on to communicate through any situation.

I am certain the principles that I lay out in this book have improved EVERY aspect of my life! How certain am I that they will help you too? How about this? If, at the end of this book, you feel like I didn't make good on that promise, contact me and I will buy it back from you.

You literally have nothing to lose, and EVERYTHING to gain. Welcome to Training Day!

TRAINING PHASE 1

The Problem

Chapter 1:

SILENCE

There are a LOT of things I miss from my childhood. Not the least of which is the reckless abandon I lived with that, apparently, I lost somewhere along the way. I mean, we used to build bicycle ramps from bricks and spare pieces of plywood so high that our hands would briefly go numb when we landed. There were no bicycle shocks in those days because we were TOUGH! Notice I said *were*. Today, I am careful when I step off the curb, because ain't nobody got time for a sprained ankle!

But a close second on the list of things I miss from my younger days is the forced downtime that was built into our technology.

Being born in 1974, I did all of my growing up in the '80s and '90s. During the '80s, whenever I had a friend spend the night, we would witness a rather strange event. We'd be watching TV, finishing off our Jiffy Pop popcorn while washing it down with a 2 liter of Big K (because who could afford Coke back then?) straight outta the bottle, when the National Anthem would begin playing on the television.

It was awkward. As a nine-year-old, I was never sure about the protocol. Do you stand when the National Anthem plays in your living room with no adults around? Could you just put your hand over your heart while you stayed sitting in your bean-bag chair? So many questions.

Flag protocols aside, we knew what happened next. It was a nightly ritual.

When the anthem was over, the station stopped broadcasting for the day. So we turned the TV off. Because back in the days before cable, once the stations stopped broadcasting the TV became useless. We didn't own a VCR at the time, and Al Gore had not yet invented the internet, so we just went to bed. There was, literally, nothing else to do.

I have no idea what time in the morning the stations began broadcasting again. I was never up early enough to watch them come back on. But there was a time when the world as I knew it went silent.

My daughters have both expressed a longing for the time in which their mother and I grew up. They know their world is a lot noisier than ours was. They know we spent 90 percent of our time outside playing with our friends because there was no other way to hang out with them. We just found stuff to do, and MOST of it was legal and didn't cause injury.

When was the last time the technology in your life was silent? Does that thought make you cringe? It bothers me. I LOVE my technology, but I kinda miss those nightly breaks from the rudimentary technology of my childhood.

Silence hits differently today because we live in a world that seems to NEVER be silent.

Silence hits differently today because we live in a world that seems to NEVER be silent.

THE THREAT OF SILENCE

The military uses a term sometimes called Radio Silence. This was used, most often, during an invasion in case the enemy was monitoring radio transmissions. I was never in the military, but I was a police officer for twenty years. I can only think of a few times where we would go *silent*:

1. When we were looking for someone who we knew had a scanner at their house (remember those things?).
2. When we were searching a business premises or a residence looking for someone we thought might be hiding from us. It was the most adrenaline-filled game of hide-and-seek ever, and we didn't want to give away our position by talking or using the radio. Using hand signals and gestures kept us safer.

You see, silence was part of our strategy. It was used intentionally in short-term, mostly adversarial situations. **Silence is a tactic**. It cannot be standard practice in our businesses.

In working with organizations today, one of my biggest pet peeves is when a company goes Radio Silent during the worst time possible. A product doesn't live up to expectations … silence. An employee is embroiled in a public scandal …

silence. Profits are down, morale is low … and my supervisor is silent.

I know.

These are difficult situations.

We don't know what to say, and so too many times, we say nothing.

But silence without rapport feels like we don't care. Deployed in the wrong situations, it will have detrimental effects.

Silence without rapport feels like we don't care.

If we are on different *teams*, silence makes sense. Let's say we both sell donuts. (You didn't think you could read a book written by a cop without talking about donuts, did you?) You don't want me to know your secret recipe, and I don't expect you to share your marketing plans with me. We're not on the same team.

However, the unfortunate side effect of silence in the *wrong* place, is that it tends to inadvertently FORM teams. If we work together and you are silent with me, I may start to assume that I am somehow on a different team.

Let's say we work together at the same donut shop. If you don't tell me when you changed the schedule, or what's in the new flavor of the month, or how many maple bars Mrs. Jones likes in her Wednesday baker's dozen and she's upset when I filled the order wrong, then I am going to start to believe we are somehow on a different team. I might wonder if you're out to get me. Do you see the potential divisiveness silence can create?

The human brain most often interprets silence as a threat, activating the fight or flight response. I know. That makes ZERO sense. But that's the problem with our brain sometimes. When it interprets something as a threat, it never makes it out of the *lizard brain*—a.k.a. the R-complex (reptilian complex). And when something stays in the lizard brain, it means it bypassed EVERY logical portion of our brain.

While calmly reading this book, you can think through the busy morning at the donut shop and understand that there's probably a logical explanation for the silence. Maybe you simply forgot about the schedule change and didn't realize you wouldn't be there to fill Mrs. Jones's special order yourself. But in the moment, when Mrs. Jones is storming out of the bakery after yelling at me in front of a line of customers, logic wasn't invited to the party. Logic ran to the backroom to mindlessly scroll Instagram in an attempt to escape the embarrassment. The only thing left is the lizard brain, and it has ZERO time for logic. It's ALL survival, ALL the time. Logic takes too long when you're running from a saber tooth tiger. Logic comes in later.

Why is silence often seen as a threat? Because of the difference between situational and dispositional attribution. Those are fancy-sounding words, and I feel super smart for including them in this book, but they are simple concepts.

Situational attribution is when we infer that someone's actions are a result of their situation (external factors). Meaning, when my boss isn't getting back to me in a timely manner, it's probably because she is busy, or her assistant didn't relay the message, or maybe she died. Probably not that last one, but you never know.

Dispositional attribution is when we infer that someone's actions are a result of their disposition (internal factors). When my boss doesn't get back to me promptly, it's
probably because she doesn't like me. Why doesn't she like
me? Am I about to get fired? Ugh! It's probably because of
that dumb thing I said at that Christmas party two years
ago. I mean, who says "Merry Christmas ya filthy animal!"
when their boss wishes them a merry Christmas? That's yet
ANOTHER time that Macaulay Culkin has led me astray.
I'm beginning to understand why that kid was left alone
so often! So now I'm being fired (insert screaming into the
mirror with both hands on my face because you can't have
enough *Home Alone* references).

Here's the problem. Without enough rapport built up, our
brain will default to interpret silence as a dispositional attribution. Without an explanation as to WHY someone important
to us is silent, our brain alerts us to an imagined threat. While
in reality, their silence is more than likely a situational attribution. They got busy. Our message got buried. Or we sent only
an attachment, so the email went into their spam folder. Any
one of these could have caused the problem. That is the logical
explanation. But remember, perceived threats don't get the benefit of logic.

Perceived threats don't get the benefit of logic.

When I present this material in person, I start with thirty
seconds of silence. After the host introduces me and turns the
mic over to me, I say nothing. For thirty seconds.

Put your finger on this page. Close the book. Look at your watch (or phone if you are under forty years old) and just be silent for thirty seconds.

I'll wait.

That was a long time, wasn't it?

Maybe you couldn't do it. You looked at your phone, and after fifteen seconds of silence, you started scrolling social media.

It was just too awkward!

If you have seen me present this content live, you would have experienced how long thirty seconds actually is. If you have not seen me do this live, you're just going to have to trust me.

On a stage, when people expect me to say something, silence gets awkward after about ten seconds. It starts getting painful around the twenty-second mark. On more than one occasion, someone in the audience has attempted to fill the silence.

They have asked if I'm okay.

They have cracked a joke.

And the clearing of throats, the mumbled exchanges between neighbors, and the squeak of conference chairs as people wrestle with the discomfort of the situation is always entertaining to me.

When my thirty-second alarm sounds, I say something like,

> "That was only thirty seconds. You expected me to say something, and I didn't. The ball was clearly in my court, and I did nothing with it. Sitting on the other end of my silence was VERY uncomfortable for a lot of you. How long have your employees or customers been waiting to hear from you? How uncomfortable are they?"

I have had more than one business leader come up to me after the presentation and tell me that they had no idea how damaging their silence was until they sat there for thirty seconds waiting for me to say something. In those thirty seconds, their brain came up with dozens of potential reasons for my silence. None of which, at that moment, made them think the two hours spent in this presentation would be beneficial.

One executive endorsed my presentation by saying, "Excellent guest speaker at our annual training for project managers. His presentation provided a much-needed promotion to improving communication within our organization. Over 20 years of exposure to leadership training, and he provided a message that I had not heard before."

So there's the good news. If you have been silent in your organization, like I am at the start of my presentations, you CAN recover. You can fix it. Rapport can be established or rebuilt at any time. Rapport is the secret sauce.

Rapport is the secret sauce.

Rapport is what allows my wife and I to be silent on car trips for an hour or more, and neither one of us feels like the other one is angry about something. Neither one of us is mad. We're simply comfortable with the level of our relationship. But that rapport is based on tens of thousands of hours of conversation. Rapport (in this example, love) was cultivated through conversations and time spent together. Rapport is the bridge that will support the weight of silence.

Rapport will prevent our silence being perceived as a threat. When people get to know our character, they will be more likely to give us the benefit of the doubt.

WHY WE SHUT DOWN UNDER STRESS

If silence is so damaging to organizations, why do so many businesses shut down communication during a crisis? That's a great question, and I have a theory. The best way I can explain that theory is by telling you about the day I watched my youngest daughter almost die right in front of me due to my ignorance.

In order for this story to make sense, the first thing you need to know about me is that I am not very *outdoorsy*. I mean, I like being outside, but I also like air conditioning. So, I'll hike, I'll play outside, I'll go for a walk, but I'm not interested in tent camping. If you have an air-conditioned RV with a fridge and a shower, I'll consider it.

I don't fish, and I don't hunt. Now, don't get me wrong, I will eat whatever you catch or kill. I just don't have the desire to catch or kill it myself when the grocery store or restaurant will do all that work for me. Basically, I'm not going to survive for long abandoned in the woods by myself. And I'm okay with that. But I am also a guy, so I spend a lot of my time pretending I am a bit manlier than I actually am.

I felt your eye roll when you read that. Cut me some slack. I have issues.

But I digress.

A few years ago, while my oldest daughter was at church camp, my youngest daughter, who was thirteen years old at the time, had expressed an interest in kayaking. At the time, we were trying to get her to do ANYTHING that did not involve her phone in front of her face, so I was excited about this newfound kayaking desire. My wife's brother has all the necessary gear, and the creek that runs through our county is perfect for kayaking, but only after a big rain.

So that day, after a good summertime thunderstorm, we decided to borrow his equipment to take our daughter kayaking. Now, neither my wife nor I had ever been kayaking before, but we had been canoeing. How hard can it be, right? There's that pretending thing that men sometimes do. We were in my brother-in-law's barn loading up the kayaks, and I was only half-listening to his instructions about obstacles in the creek. Not paying attention almost cost my daughter's life. But more on that later.

As we were loading up, he said, "The life jackets are over there."

I looked at him funny, and said, "The creek is waist deep at BEST. We don't need life jackets."

My wife quickly chimed in and assured me that ALL of us would be wearing life jackets. After 20-plus years of marriage, you learn when to fight, and when not to. It was hot outside, but I knew the creek was mostly in the shade, so I didn't dig in. I grabbed a life jacket because my wife is not just another pretty face. She's smart too!

When we got to the creek and pushed off in our kayaks, I was surprised by how fast the water was moving. This was going to be fun, and I wasn't sweating too bad under my life jacket. I even pulled my cell phone out of the waterproof lanyard and took a picture of the Harvey Kayak Trip for Instagram, because if you don't post when you do cool things as a parent, how do you expect to make the other parents jealous of your picture-perfect life?

We thought it would be safest, that day, if my wife went first, Maryn was second, and I brought up the rear. Each of us stayed about 30 yards apart. We navigated the creek pretty easily, and we laughed a lot. It was a good day until…

I heard the water rushing before we rounded the bend in the creek. Once I could see around the corner, I saw that two trees had fallen across the water. One from either side. At that point, I remembered my brother-in-law saying something about this. He said something like, "The trees are blocking most of the creek, but my wife and I go around it all the time. It's no big deal." Not being Mr. Outdoors, I did not know that "go around it" meant paddling to the bank, getting out, carrying your kayak *around* the partial dam created by the trees, and putting it safely back in the water on the other side of the obstruction.

When I saw the trees had a kayak-sized gap in-between them, my brain figured "go around them" meant with a few turns, you could paddle around them. Turns out it WAS possible … just not smart. An important distinction, I would learn.

My wife went first, and after two BEAUTIFUL 180-degree turns, she safely navigated the gap between the trees even in the rushing water.

Maryn was next. Now, at thirteen, she had EXACTLY as much experience as her mother and I at kayaking, but not the arm strength. When she maneuvered into her first turn, she turned a little too late, and her kayak washed sideways against the first tree. Those of you with any kayaking experience or basic knowledge of physics know what came next. Her kayak caught the rushing water broadside and rolled under the tree taking the boat and the teenager underwater. Right before she went under, she LOCKED eyes with me.

I was about thirty yards behind her. And then she was gone. Her boat popped right back up on the other side of the tree, but she did not. In a split second, I was standing in the waist-deep water and wading as fast as I could toward where I had last seen her. And I still couldn't find her. Her boat was floating away, and she was missing.

I got about halfway to the tree before spotting her elbow. It was the only thing sticking above the water. Her arm was wrapped around the upstream tree as she held on for dear life. I briefly saw her face rise above the water. She gasped for air and went back under. I moved toward her and realized I would only have one chance at this. The water was rushing so quickly that if I got washed past where she was holding on, I didn't think I could fight the current to make it back to her.

Thankfully, the next thing I registered was finding myself standing, firmly planted right next to where she was underwater. I grabbed her by the shoulders of her life jacket (that I didn't think we needed), and I pulled with everything in me. She came out from under the tree and started coughing and crying at the same time. When she coughed, water came gushing out of her mouth and nose. I've never seen anything scarier.

My kayak floated up at about this time, so I told her to get in my boat, and I would walk her to her kayak while she regained her composure. Once she settled down a little, she looked at me and said, "I just kept telling myself, Daddy's coming. Daddy's coming." Those two words almost broke me. She KNOWS me. She knows I'm not outdoorsy. But she also knew that I would do ANYTHING to save her.

I walked that boat about a hundred yards downstream to where my wife had gathered Maryn's kayak. We finished the trip without incident, but my daughter has ZERO interest in a career in kayaking. I have assured her there was no money in a kayaking career these days, anyway.

When we got home, my wife and daughter hit the showers to wash the creek off. I sat on the front porch, drank a beer, and tried to deal with the adrenaline dump of almost watching my daughter drown in front of me on a beautiful summer day due to my ignorance.

That's when it hit me. Her kayak washed under the tree with no problem. The only reason she didn't was because she grabbed a hold of the tree. Her lizard brain detected danger and sent one message to the rest of her body, "Hold on. Daddy's coming." Had she not held on, she would have washed downstream without incident. By holding on to something that FELT safe and strong, her feet washed out from under her, and she was unable to stand. The rushing water going under the tree kept her submerged ONLY because she was holding on.

You see, when her whole world turned upside down, she reached for the first *safe* thing she could find, and she held onto it with all her might. And that is what almost killed her. On my front porch, I realized that, logically, letting go of the tree was what Maryn should have done, and she understands that now. But logic doesn't get a vote when survival is on the line.

When things get scary for an organization, when things turn upside down, we grab a hold of silence, and we hang on … because it FEELS safe. We start to feel like we can't breathe, and so we hold on tighter because we don't know what else to do. It's quite possible that what you are holding onto is what is keeping you stuck. In a post-COVID world, what worked before is not going to work now. We let go of a LOT of stuff during 2020. And, in my experience, the organizations that weathered the storm of the pandemic the best were the ones that chose to overcommunicate. The organizations that were already great at communicating never missed a beat. Those who didn't prioritize communication in 2019 either closed in 2020 or started communicating with their employees and their customers like never before.

Your organization is not the exception.

Your silence is costing you more than you realize, but it doesn't have to stay that way.

Effective communication Is the necessary commodity for any successful organization today. You don't lack ability or desire. You only lack training and confidence.

Every athlete I know trains before they go into their first game. Every police officer has THOUSANDS of hours of training before confronting their first emergency. Applying the principles in this book will give you the skills you need to break the silence and move your organization, your leadership, and your career forward.

How do we best break the silence? We'll get there, I promise. Before we get too far into tactics, we need to spend some time understanding how the brain processes communication. After all, it does not matter what you say or how you say it if others cannot receive it. Let's talk about strategies to make sure our message can be heard.

Chapter 2:

THE BRAIN

My brain is broken. I caused it. I didn't mean to, but I broke it. You see, as a police officer for 20 years, I rewired my brain. You know how you assume everything will work out, people are inherently good, you rarely question people's motives, and you are surprised when the worst possible scenario comes to pass? That's so cute about you. Don't lose that. That's a great way to go through life, but it's not conducive to survival in the world of law enforcement. I wish that statement wasn't true.

I would love to tell you that the cynical police officer stereotype isn't a thing, but it is. And, to be fair, we deal most frequently with the 5% of the population that commits most of the crimes. When we deal with the other 95%, it's on their worst day of the year.

No one calls the police when things are going well. No one calls 911 to report that they got a new job, their husband washed the dishes without being asked, and their kids made the honor roll. We are not the *celebrators*. We are the *clean-up crew*. We get called in when there is a mess, so we forget that life isn't as messy as it seems to us. We spend our time day in and day out immersed in everyone's mess, and that breaks our brains.

More scientifically, that reprograms our Reticular Activating System (RAS). The RAS is the data input filter for our brain. Every sight, sound, smell, physical touch or sensation comes through the RAS first. Each one of us is exposed to SO MUCH input that it would overwhelm our brain if it all made it through. How much input? How about around eleven million bits per second. The problem is our brains can only consciously process about 50 bits per second.

My wife and I taught both of our daughters to drive when they turned sixteen. The very first driving lesson always reminded me how much we are actually DOING when we drive a car. Most of it isn't even a conscious thought, so I would forget to break it down for my daughters. Things like how much pressure to apply to the pedals (sore necks from the quick stops and starts are to be expected in the beginning), how quickly or slowly to turn the wheel, checking lines of sight in the direction you are going without forgetting to check the mirrors periodically to make sure you are aware of what's coming up behind you, ignoring the vibrating cell phone, listening to the directions from your phone (because teenagers know where NOTHING is located because they spent the last several years watching their phone screens in the car instead of developing the mental maps we had as teenagers), skipping songs you don't want to hear to get to the JAMS … and we still manage to be surprised by the cost of insuring teen drivers? The input is overwhelming. I'm exhausted just typing it!

The RAS is the filter that keeps us alive and SANE by only allowing things through that it deems important. It shields us from about 11,999,950 bits of input per second. Now would be a great time to thank your RAS for the job it is doing!

Now that you're an experienced driver, or a *professional driver* as I repeatedly assure my wife when she sucks all the oxygen out of the car because I MAY have gotten a little close to another car, you don't think about every sensation and sound while you drive. I highly doubt that you're reciting "signal, mirror, over the shoulder and go" every time you pull out.

So, how does the RAS know what bits to let through the filter? Basically, we tell it what's important by what we focus on.

Let's take a concrete look at the RAS at work. Think about the last time that you bought a new (or new-to-you) car. As soon as you drove your new car off the lot, I bet you started noticing that same model vehicle EVERYWHERE. You became convinced that a lot of people had run out and bought the EXACT same car as you. Seriously? Show some originality, people! You bought this car to be DIFFERENT, and now it's not so different.

Here's the crazy part: Those cars were there all the time. They simply didn't make it through the filter because they were unimportant. They were background noise that your RAS filtered out for you. By picking the car you did, investing money in it, and assigning some of your identity to it, your RAS labeled it *important*, and let it through the *noise*.

After 20 years as a police officer, my RAS is really good at letting things through that might get me hurt. My RAS is skewed toward threats. I notice things that *don't belong* or people acting *strangely*. And, in case you are wondering, there are a LOT of people acting strangely today. I start to see everything as a threat

Want to spot an off-duty police officer in a restaurant? Look for the person sitting at a table, probably against the wall, who is facing the door (or the room as a whole), and glancing up every time someone walks in. Congratulations. You found the cop! Why? Because we are conditioned to be aware of our surroundings. And in an off-duty capacity, it is very possible that the next person through the door could be someone that cop arrested recently. We want to see them before they see us.

We constantly run scenarios in our head to plan a strategy— just in case. We also consciously map out where the closest exit is to us, what in the room would offer concealment (hide us), or what we could use for cover (to stop a bullet) in an emergency.

Sound exhausting? Welcome to the law enforcement brain. It's conditioned for survival, and it is VERY difficult to turn that part off.

BE READY TO SAY *SOMETHING*

As a public information officer for my agency, my brain also runs scenarios about how I would explain this situation to the press, if I had to. I was the one called in to any major accident or crime to talk with the media. My job was to tell the public what we could while protecting innocent victim's (and everyone's) civil rights. At the same time, I needed to minimize false rumors and accusations. I was a professional storyteller. When I work with businesses today, I help them tell their story and control the message.

My brain has gotten very good at this over my 20-year career. I quickly learned that the first person to tell the story controls the narrative. Even when the story would make you or your company look bad, ESPECIALLY when it could make you look bad, you NEED to be the first one telling the story.

The first person to tell the story controls the narrative.

We all mess up. Be honest. If something didn't turn out the way you anticipated, say that. And then tell me what you are going to do about it. Let me know that you are aware, that you care, and that you are going to correct the issue. Address any mistakes and assure your employees or customers that you have implemented changes. It will decrease the likelihood of you repeating these mistakes and is the best way to restore confidence.

As mentioned before, silence without rapport feels like we don't care. In a crisis, say SOMETHING. This does not mean that we get in debates or release multiple statements about an incident. It does mean that the first move needs to be ours.

You won't kill the story by not talking.

You WILL lose control of it by keeping silent.

Release a statement as soon as you can, and then get about fixing the problem.

This is exactly what we're going to train for. However, it's not enough just to put out a message. We also have to understand how that message will be received.

MORE THAN WORDS

(If you are now singing the song by Extreme after reading that subtitle, you are my kinda people.)

While the public information officer side of my brain runs these stories through various iterations in my head, it is the hostage negotiator side that kicks in first. You see, whenever you are communicating a message, you have to do more than simply craft the words. You also have to make sure it is going to be heard. Stephen Covey says, "Begin with the end in mind." I would encourage you to communicate with the audience in mind.

Communicate with the audience in mind.

Using brain science to our advantage, we need to make sure our message is able to get through. In my experience, there are two big hindrances to messages getting through today: Stress and Fear. These are important enough that I have dedicated a chapter to unpacking each one.

Before we get to those in detail, it's important to understand how our brains process communication. Evolutionarily speaking, our brains prefer to process communication in a face-to-face mode. When you think about it, that was the ONLY way our early ancestors could communicate. And since evolution is a SLOW process, that is still our preferred method of communicating. We rely on context cues to interpret the whole message.

Researchers have actually studied how our brains process communication and they found that we only get 7% of the message from the actual words someone says. Which begs the question, what makes up the other 93%? That's a GREAT question, and understanding the answer will revolutionize how you communicate.

Our brains pull about 38% of the message from the tone (how does someone say what they are saying: volume, cadence, etc.), and the other 55% from nonverbal cues (eye movements, facial expressions, arm gestures, hand movements, leg crossing, posture, etc.). This creates a LOT of confusion in a world that has all but abandoned face-to-face communication, as you can imagine.

I'm sure I'm not the only one who's wondering if I'm in the doghouse after a text exchange like this with my significant other:

Thought I would go out for supper with the guys tonight after work.

That's fine

Graphic by Grace Harvey

"Thought I would go out for supper with the guys after work today."

"That's fine."

Hmmm… is that:

"Fine, no problem. I'm busy and hadn't even thought about supper yet. Have fun!"

It MIGHT be.

Or is it:

"That's fine! I guess I'll just eat some of this supper I prepared on my own, and you can warm yours up for lunch tomorrow, if you can grace us with your presence long enough."

Ouch.

It's AMAZING how many nuanced meanings the two simple words "that's fine" can have. You need the tone and/or nonverbal cues to know for sure.

If you've ever had someone mad at you for a text or a social media post, and you can't figure out how they could POSSIBLY be offended by what you wrote, just ask them to read it out loud to you. When they read it with THEIR tone, it will become abundantly clear as to why they are angry. You typed it with your tone, and it was witty, or sarcastic, or whatever. When they read it back to you, with their tone, it's easy to see why they are upset.

When I talk about this with my teenage daughter, she rolls her eyes and says, "That's what emojis are for, dad!" And emojis DO help communicate tone, but I wouldn't recommend using them in professional work emails or client texts.

If we want to tell our story, we must make sure our message can be heard. We have to speak up if we're going to break through the RAS filter. We have to acknowledge how important tone and nonverbal cues are, and the risks of communicating without them. We also have to understand how vitally important it is to manage stress and fear—both the audience's and our own. And that means silence isn't the only problem.

Chapter 3:
STRESS

As a hostage negotiator, I never got a chance to communicate with someone who was NOT under stress. When you are dealing with someone who doesn't feel living is worth the fight anymore because their family has disowned them, they keep getting arrested due to their poor choices, they cannot get a meaningful job due to their criminal record, the state has custody of all of their kids due to their inability to care for them, and they are now talking to a police officer feeling like they are going to repeat the cycle all over again—stress is, understandably, through the roof.

I wish this was a description of ONE person that I spoke with as a negotiator. Sadly, this is the archetype ... only the names change.

When I wasn't at the police department, I was helping my two daughters navigate the awkwardness of middle school, which, from their perspective, can be just as stressful. I also coached them to manage their social media, taught them to hit killer float serves on the volleyball court, and tried to help them understand teenage boys' inability to adequately communicate. All of which were significant points of stress for them … my daughters … not the teenage boys. From what I could tell, the biggest stressors on these boys were girls and running out of Axe Body Spray, but I digress.

I guess you could say, in both my professional and personal life, I have had a LOT of practice communicating with people during some very stressful situations. And I know that stress is one of the biggest hindrances to effective communication today. Because, if you weren't stressed about social media, race relations, an unstable political atmosphere, or a myriad of other issues … 2020 threw a global pandemic onto everyone's plate as well!

STRESS? WHAT STRESS?

As someone who made 95% of my business income speaking to large groups, deciding as a society that gathering en masse could possibly kill us, I felt stress in a whole new way. I couldn't do what I felt I was MADE to do, and my brain didn't know how to handle this. Some of you found yourselves working from home for the first time in your life, and that was never the plan. You DID like the whole not-having-to-wear-pants thing, but eventually, the walls started closing in. It wasn't immediate. In the beginning, it was an unexpected adventure! I mean, we had never *global pandemic-ed* before!

I reached out to a professional counselor for the first time in my adult life early in 2021 and was put on a 60-day waiting list to schedule my first appointment. Apparently, I was not the only one struggling to adequately process all that 2020 threw at us.

Mental health experts saw instances of anxiety and depression spike. According to an American Psychiatric Association poll, from 2016 to 2019, around 35% of Americans felt more stressed at any given moment than they did the year before. However, when you jump to October of 2020, 62% of Americans felt more anxious than they did in October of 2019. It seems even the science shows that after "two weeks to flatten the curve" turned into "six months, and we still don't know when this will end," our brains had had enough. I know mine did.

Here's what I learned through my journey. If you have feelings of anxiety, panic, or depression, it does not mean you are *broken* or *weak*. It simply means you are exhibiting symptoms of a fairly common illness. An illness that you didn't get because you are weak, but one that a LOT of people are experiencing. And the good news is, it is an illness that is HIGHLY treatable if we can convince you that it is okay to talk about it.

Stress. Anxiety. Depression.

We don't like to talk about these, and that's not okay.

We can only heal what we are able to talk about.

I believe that one of the positive aspects of the global pandemic is that we seem to be more open than ever to having discussions about mental health. I have ALWAYS been a fan of open and honest discussions. It's the only way we improve things.

For our purposes, we need to understand the hindrance that stress creates for people who we are hoping to communicate with. It doesn't matter if we are communicating with our employees or our customers, the stress they are experiencing is like a vibration or humming in their bodies that has the ability to drown out anything you say.

If we want others to hear our message, we must help them deal with the stress first.

RIDING THE TEETER-TOTTER

One of the most useful things I learned in hostage-negotiator training is about the teeter-totter in everyone's brain. You didn't know it was there, but once I explain it to you, you will never forget it. It will radically change how you communicate.

My clearest memory of teeter-totters as a kid was leaning back and digging my heels into the ground so that I could keep whoever was on the other end suspended at the top of the tee-ter-totter. Then threatening to jump off to send them crashing back to the ground. This happened to me, or I did it to one of my friends, pretty much EVERY time we got on a teeter-totter. It was part of the game ... and probably why there aren't a lot of teeter-totters still on playgrounds today. My generation broke too many tailbones. Sorry about that.

But having grown up with teeter-totters, I understand the physics of them on a basic level. When one side is low, the other side is high. On the teeter-totter that everyone has in their brains, emotion sits on one end with logic/reason parked on the other end. So when emotion is high, the logic/reason side of our brain is low. And when I say emotion, that can be ANY emotion (fear, anger, frustration, lust, etc.). Now, this teeter-totter goes up and down pretty much all day as emotions come and go. On most days, it doesn't move enough for us to notice. But sometimes the emotional end can practically touch the sky.

Graphic by Grace Harvey

As you can imagine, when I first made contact with someone that I was called in to negotiate with, their emotions were through the roof. So, what does that mean? Well, think about the teeter-totter. When someone is experiencing a highly emotional event, they are physiologically incapable of hearing a logical solution. This is why when your spouse comes home super stressed from their day, and as they are venting you offer a calm and perfectly logical solution to their problem, they go on as if they didn't even hear you. They aren't being rude. Their teeter-totter is unbalanced. They truly are not capable of processing logic at that moment. Emotion has them trapped up high, their feet dangling wild, and absolutely sure they're going to plummet into sheer pain at any moment. But if you allow them to vent— if you ask open-ended questions and keep them talking—there's a good chance they will arrive, seemingly on their own, at the logical solution that you offered twenty minutes before. They heard it. They just couldn't process it until their teeter-totter starts to come back into balance.

If emotion was SUPER high, they may not have even heard it. But now that their feet can occasionally touch the ground, they can hear what you have to say.

This is what makes a timeout a BRILLIANT parenting hack that can also be used effectively in the workplace.

You see, when I was a kid, I thought a timeout was the worst punishment EVER. Back in my day, when you got sent to your room, it was not a lot of fun. In my room, I had a bed, a dresser, and some dirty clothes that needed to be put in the hamper. My room did not have a television. My room did not have a computer. I didn't have a smartphone to scroll TikToks while I rode out my timeout. I just sat there and stared. It was terrible!

When my kids were small, I came to realize that a timeout is not a punishment. A timeout is what kept me from killing my kids when my teeter-totter was out of balance. When my emotions were getting too high, if I was smart, I would send my kids to their rooms for a timeout. During this timeout, my teeter-totter would balance itself, and I would be better equipped to deal with the situation.

On more than one occasion, when my emotions came down, I would go into their room and apologize for losing my temper.

The times that I did not give them a timeout were too often the times when I said something that hurt them or raised my voice unnecessarily. When emotions are high, communication deteriorates quickly.

Are things getting stressful at work? Is a discussion getting heated? When you feel your emotions escalating, what if you said something like, "I do want to discuss this with you. Can you give me 15 minutes to take care of something first?" If you spend those 15 minutes bringing your teeter-totter back into balance, I promise you when you resume that difficult conversation, things will go better.

Because of my training in hostage negotiations, and being naive enough to believe that kindness matters, I always thought about this teeter-totter when I was dealing with someone on the street. As you can imagine, I got called a lot of unflattering names. I got threatened. I even had people try to fight me. But I also grew up watching Patrick Swayze play Dalton in *Road House*.

Go ahead and name a cooler character in a movie, I'll wait.

One of the things that Dalton said repeatedly when he trained the bouncers in the bar he was hired to turn around, was to "*Be nice.*" If they had to kick someone out, he said, "Ask him to walk, but be nice. If he won't walk, walk him, but be nice. If you can't walk him, one of the others will help, and you will both be nice. I want you to remember that it's the job. It's nothing personal." As a police officer, I learned that I could nicely arrest someone. I could nicely take someone to the ground who was wanting to fight me. I could tell someone no in a nice way, and I could nicely talk my way out of MOST fights.

More times than not, the person I arrested, who threatened me, called me names, and fought me … apologized at the jail when their teeter-totter righted itself. When the stress wore off, they *came to their senses*, realized they were a big jerk, and I had been nice when I didn't have to be.

I can't tell you the times that I ran into people I had arrested when I was off duty and had my young daughters with me, and they were nice to me and my family because I had *nicely* arrested them. Be nice!

BRING BACK BALANCE

Since there is a REALLY good chance that you will not be negotiating for the lives of hostages or arresting anyone today, you may be wondering where the application is for you.

I'm betting that you have team members whose teeter-totters may be a little out of balance.

You have clients and customers who are experiencing some type of emotion when you contact them.

And if they have contacted you, the chance that their teeter-totter is out of balance goes up exponentially.

Most of the time, if a customer or client is reaching out to you, it is because they have a problem. If they are a new customer, they are contacting you because they have a problem that they are hoping you can help them solve. If they are an existing customer, they may be having a problem with your product or service ... something they have PAID you for. That's kind of emotional.

Ryan Serhant, star of *Million Dollar Listing New York* and best-selling author, preaches all the time that buying is ALWAYS an emotional event. It is not a logical thing. If you are selling a product or service, you are dealing with emotions on a transaction-by-transaction basis. So our job, then, becomes helping someone navigate the emotions we know they are feeling.

Are they scared? What information can you give them to reassure them this purchase is right for them?

Are they feeling pressured to buy NOW? Can you give them information about the availability of the product that might lower the emotion side of their teeter-totter?

Are their emotions clouding their judgment? How can you help them talk through these emotions so that logic and reason can play a part in their decision as well?

If we can get them to approach their decision with an equal mix of logic and emotion, they will leave that transaction feeling better about how we treated them. We recognized the emotions of the process, but we also helped them bring logic into their decision.

Oftentimes, the real challenge is not allowing their imbalanced teeter-totter to unbalance your own. You can recognize emotion without answering with your own high emotion. That being said, it's not super helpful to bring ONLY logic and reason to an emotional situation either.

In my opinion, one of the biggest challenges facing law enforcement as a profession is that we tend to operate more on logic and reason than emotion. That helps us make better decisions under stress, but it also makes us come across very cold and unfeeling. Remember what we learned in Chapter 2: Silence without rapport feels like we don't care. We in law enforcement are tasked with making HIGH-STRESS, split-second decisions to save our lives or that of an innocent victim. There's not a lot of room for emotion in that situation. We need to act quickly. But we don't need to operate with the emotion side of our tee-ter-totter always buried in the sand. There is a time for logic and reason, but it can't be ALL the time.

As I mentioned before, part of the fun of a teeter-totter for the kid in me is jumping off one end to watch your friend come crashing down to earth; because gravity isn't just a good idea … it's the LAW.

I believe in law enforcement we need to spend a LOT more time with the emotion side of our brain showing. When a threat appears, we can push hard on the ground from the logic and reason side allowing emotions to crash to the earth while logic and reason shoot up to deal with the threat. Once the threat is handled, we can allow emotion to come back up.

It happens in civilian life too. Nothing frustrates me more than calling tech support for most companies. After pressing 2, 5, 7, 4, giving my dog's birthday, promising my firstborn child, and screaming, "SPEAK TO A REPRESENTATIVE!", a live person finally comes on the line. Then I state my problem only to hear the person on the other end typing it into their computer, and answer me with a flat, robotic, "I am sorry to hear you are having this issue." You're not sorry. You're reading a script. Which is a REALLY good way to make me even more upset!

Apple Support has solved this problem. There are some days I want to call them even when I don't have a problem. Because I know I will get a REAL human who is not reading a script, and genuinely wants to help. One of the last times I called Apple Support, when I told them what was happening with my MacBook, the Apple employee on the other end said, "That sucks, man. It shouldn't be doing that, but it's a fairly easy fix. I'll talk you through the process." A perfect balance of emotion, "That sucks," and logic and reason, "I'll talk you through the process." Brilliant!

Understanding stress and how it drowns out even the best of messages is key. But it's not the only barrier. As a negotiator, I learned that our emotions drive our fears, and it is our fears that keep us from being able to balance our teeter-totters.

Chapter 4:

FEAR

I f 2020 and 2021 had a commodity they were selling, I'm pretty sure it was fear. Every day there was something else to be afraid of. We did not want to appear racist, or privileged, or xenophobic, or misogynistic, or too woke, or uncaring, or other VALID issues all while wearing our mask appropriately and maintaining six feet of social distance between us and the WORLD ... because, Global Pandemic. I mean, if you didn't offend anyone in 2020 or 2021, it's because you didn't say anything. And if you were one of the *silent* ones, it's still possible the internet trolls dug out some obscure tweet of yours from 15 years ago that is *offensive* today. It was an all-out Offensive Scavenger Hunt, and we were quick to publicly shame those that crossed the line all while moving the line so that no one knew exactly where it was safe to step.

But in reality, we quit communicating effectively due to fear LONG before the global pandemic. We became so afraid of saying the WRONG thing, that we felt it was safer to say NOTHING. If you remember, silence without rapport feels like we don't care. So in the midst of a lot of turmoil, a lot of organizations came off as cold and uncaring simply because they were trying not to offend anyone. Basically, in an effort to not offend people, we offend people.

IT'S PERSONAL. EVEN IN BUSINESS.

I am not casting stones here. This is a tumultuous time, for sure. We walk on eggshells to get anywhere today. I get it. But all too often our silence comes off more as uncaring than trying not to accidentally say the wrong thing. In my experience, it is easier to apologize in an ongoing conversation than it is to wade into a conversation LONG after it has started. Because when we are silent, our audience (customers, clients, and employees) will attribute our silence to our disposition instead of our situation, and we will struggle to recover.

Fear Keeps Us Silent

Imagine you're at a conference and sitting near the back of the room—because that's where the cool kids sit—when the guy on stage (me) asks for a volunteer. You smile and point to your coworker who stuck you with the dinner bill last night because payback is SWEET! Little do you know, when I am not on stage, I am YOU. I am the master of volunteering other people and calling the cell phones of those who can't seem to silence them. Sometimes, like today, that mischievousness backfires.

Your movement and eye contact told me you are EXACTLY the type of person who will make this part of my presentation amazing! You play hard to get, but I know you will have no problem helping me out for a few minutes. You were MADE for the stage! So I call you to come on up.

Once on stage, I explain that your only job is to describe the next slide to the audience. "Pretend the audience can't see it. Paint a picture for them." With your high verbal skills and your mischievousness (evidenced by trying to volunteer someone else), I know you are going to KILL this! The catch is—I get to play the part of your *inner dialogue*. You know, the voice that runs through your head whenever you're making a public statement? My job is to make sure you don't offend anyone. We can't have you saying anything that will bring Will Smith out of the audience to smack you.

The slide is a picture of an older, dark-skinned gentleman wearing a hat. It's a beautiful portrait of a man who looks like someone I would love to sit and sip coffee with while he tells me about his life. The lines on his face, the fact that his mouth is SLIGHTLY turned up at the corners as if he always knows a good joke, and the gleam in his eyes tells me this man's life hasn't been easy, but his spirit is strong, and I KNOW he has stories! But describing his face to a room full of people is difficult.

Whenever I do this exercise, my volunteer (victim) usually begins by saying something to the effect of, "Well, it's an older gentleman." I cut them off by saying something like, "Older? Older than what? We can't afford to be seen as ageist here. Tread carefully! Besides, we don't KNOW that it's a gentleman. I mean, there's a mustache, but we didn't ask their preferred pronouns or gender. We can't make assumptions here." Their squirming intensifies.

Then they start to describe the hat … because that's the *safest* thing in the pic. Because they are afraid of saying the wrong thing, I have made them afraid to describe this beautiful gentleman. Their fear renders them mute VERY quickly. In all the times I have done this exercise, NO ONE has ever described his complexion. Race is the ultimate hot button issue today.

After I let my volunteer off the hook, I ask the room, "What if this gentleman was touring your facility with his family and came up missing? What if they told you he had dementia and they needed to find him right away? How would you describe him to your team? Would the exigent circumstances make you less afraid to offend in order to be more descriptive?"

Here's the rub: the more we try to tap-dance around some perceived hot-button issue, the more awkward we make things. The more awkward something becomes, the more offensive it will be. In a nutshell, in an effort to *not* offend anyone, we tend to be more offensive because we call attention to those things that we are trying not to say.

Are we going to make mistakes? Yes. Are those mistakes fatal? No. We need to be honest in our communication and speak from the heart. I have learned it is not our WORDS that offend as much as it is the HEART behind them. It is a selfish or malicious intent that can do the most damage.

Show that you—or the organization you represent—have a compassionate heart, are willing to learn, but will not shy away from important discussions, and you will do just fine navigating the *politically correct minefield* of today. Rest assured, this paragraph just offended some people. It's not my intent, but probably the result, nonetheless. Ignorance does not offend most people. Malice always does.

Don't Let Fear Sideline You

We were confronted with this whenever we trained CPR/First Aid at the police department. One of the main things that stops people from doing CPR, even if they are trained, is fear. They are afraid of hurting someone or *doing it wrong*. In training, we were constantly reminded that we were doing CPR on dead people. By definition, when you do not have a heartbeat, you are dead. It's possible to *undead* you with CPR, but it's not possible to *more dead* you at that point. Will you break the person's ribs? Maybe. Probably. But they are dead. They don't care. If you manage to *undead* them, we can fix their ribs. So have at it! There's nothing to be afraid of … except inaction. Inaction will keep them dead, for sure.

There's nothing to be afraid of … except inaction.

REFRAME THE FEAR

When you feel fear creeping into your decision-making process, you may need to reframe the situation. What's the WORST that can happen?

Let's say that you make purple widgets. Out of the blue, one day, you discover your product is breaking when the customer uses it for the first time. What's the worst that can happen?

Will customers be upset? Of course. All of them were upset when the widget you sold them failed.

Will you need to offer a refund or put out a safety recall? Probably.

Will that hurt revenue numbers for this quarter? Yes.

Will we be able to bounce back? That depends.

Let's talk through the first scenario. What will staying silent do?

When you become aware of the problem, if you try to keep it inside the company, will your customers still have failing widgets? Yes.

And now with no ownership of the problem or any replacement offered, what may have been unintentional will appear to many as cheap production used to make a quick buck by sneaking an inferior product under the radar.

Some customers will just toss the product and quietly decide not to do business with you.

Others will return it and demand a refund.

And many will leave angry reviews. Some people take GREAT delight in leaving negative reviews.

In the silent scenario, not one customer comes out happy with your product or your company. Revenue starts dropping. You need to find new customers and hope they don't read the negative reviews. Your competitor is taking more and more of the business, and sales continue their downward trend.

This is next to impossible to recover from.

Now, let's talk through the other scenario. What could happen if you speak up? What if you own this, and decide to communicate your way through this problem?

You release a statement that informs your customers of a production flaw with the purple widgets, and you offer them clear instructions on how they can get a replacement or refund.

Will customers be upset? Sure. Many were already upset when the widget failed.

Will people ask for a refund? Yes. That's a reasonable request when a product fails.

Will some people still relish leaving a negative review? Probably.

However, others will appreciate the honesty and your willingness to fix the problem. They will note this in their reviews. These customers are not lost for good. They may decide to give you another chance because we all make mistakes.

This quarter's revenue takes a hit, but you can bounce back because you spoke up and owned the problem. You apologized for the inconvenience. You offered refunds or replacements. And you built trust. You created an opportunity to retain several customers and rebuild your reputation for excellent products and great customer service.

When you work through to the worst that can happen, which scenario sounds better in the long run?

I'll pick the opportunity to bounce back any day of the week!

Can you mess things up by taking action and speaking up? Sure. But staying silent will only continue to erode trust and reputation. Taking action looks like you care. Inaction makes you look apathetic.

Fear is real.

But so is courage.

I felt fear a LOT as a police officer, but it didn't stop me from acting. My training had shown me how to act when everyone else was unsure of what to do next.

Recognize the fear. Label it. And then take appropriate action even though you are afraid.

When I was little, I thought police officers were heroes. I never really interacted with them, but I had never had a conversation with Batman either, so I didn't see this as strange. I knew they were out there making the world safer, and I dug that as a kid. I wanted that.

But as someone who has worn a hero's uniform for most of my adult life, I can assure you, it is not what a person wears that makes them a hero. Some officers have no business wearing the uniform, and a LOT of heroes don't wear any kind of uniform at all. Regardless of what you wear to work, you can be a hero.

TRAINING PHASE 2

The Solution

Chapter 5:

RAPPORT

Phase one of any training is learning to identify the problems: silence is deadly, and fear and stress stand in the way of showing up. Phase one is done.

Congratulations.

Now it's time to move into Phase 2: Identify the Solution

It's time to learn the action steps that will help us break the silence—to speak up in SPITE of our fear.

We're tempted to think that communication is all about crafting a message, choosing a good layout, or the right filter, and having a sharp-looking brand with just the right colors. But the truth is, speaking up with confidence is all about building solid skills. It has little to do with templates and color palettes. Sure, good branding will help people recognize your organization. The right look will help capture attention and stop the scroll. I mean, a sweet picture or an awesome video will get my attention every time. But the only way you are going to KEEP that attention and have your message heard is with these three skills:

1. Building Genuine Rapport
2. Listening Like it's Your Superpower
3. Choosing Words Wisely

As a police officer, I have been called to more than one scene where a driver missed a bridge. Those wrecks never worked out well. That bridge is there to provide a SAFE crossing over a chasm that would be hard to cross otherwise—with the exception, maybe, of Bo and Luke Duke. Those Duke boys always seemed to have the perfect dirt ramp to launch the General Lee when they needed it. But the rest of us best stick to the bridges.

Bridges transport us safely from one side to the other. If we are going to have our message heard, we've got to build a bridge over stress and fear. And the BEST way to do that is by putting people first.

When serving as a hostage negotiator, my MAIN job was to build rapport. The SWAT team wasn't worried about rapport. They were focused on Special Weapons and Tactics (as the name SWAT implies). Some of you just learned the meaning of an acronym that you may have never thought about before. You're welcome. I'm always trying to add value.

Rapport was my commodity as a negotiator … or a police officer in general. I spent a career convincing people to do what I needed them to do all the while thinking it was their idea. This sounds manipulative, and it can be if used improperly. However, if what I wanted them to do was what was BEST for them, I could justify it.

Skills are neutral. How we use them determines whether we are a hero or a villain.

Build rapport ONLY for the sake of making a sale, and you will come off as manipulative. You may make that sale, but they will likely not be back because of how you made them feel.

Build rapport because it helps you understand your customer, so that you can serve them better, and they'll come back to you again and again—and tell their friends as well.

We do business at the speed of rapport.

I believe that we do business at the speed of rapport. People tend to do business with organizations that they like, know, and trust. Getting someone to like, know, and trust us is pretty much the working definition of rapport. (Some of you just Googled the definition of rapport to see how close I was ... Trust, but verify!)

Think about it, when you are faced with a difficult decision, who do you bounce it off? Strangers? People you don't like? People with zero experience with the type of decision you are faced with?

No.

You take your problem to people you know. People whose opinions matter to you.

You follow advice from those you trust; those who have successfully navigated the waters you find yourself in.

I use my hostage negotiation training EVERY day. I mean, my wife and I have raised two daughters through their

teenage years. We have nerves of STEEL, and we have negotiated a LOT!

But, in all seriousness, this works in the business world as
well. We need to be building rapport ALL the time. We need to
understand our people—and by *people*, I mean our clients, our
customers, and our team members.

We need to know their fears and their goals.

We need to understand their motivations.

We need to speak their language.

And most of all, we need to demonstrate with our words
and actions that we want them to succeed.

When you begin with seeking to help people, rapport is a
natural byproduct. You will never be able to manipulate your
way to long-term success. But you can become VERY successful
when you help other people get what's best for them.

Zig Ziglar often said, "You can have everything in life you
want, if you will just help other people get what they want."

THAT's rapport!

But be warned, when we establish rapport with someone, we
open ourselves up to sharing their pain. This can be a lot to carry.

SHARED CRISIS: THE FAST TRACK

One hot, humid summer afternoon, I received a phone call
from the patrol supervisor. A small child had been pulled,
unconscious, from our local pool and transported to the hospital. The patrol supervisor was concerned that the media would
show up wanting to cover this sad summer story. As a public
information officer, I got called whenever the media might be
involved in an incident.

I arrived at the hospital and went inside to check on the victim. I found myself standing in the emergency room with the little girl's mom. Just down the hall, behind a glass wall, the doctors and nurses were working tirelessly to save her seven-year-old daughter. I quietly asked the mom how she was holding up.

"She didn't even want to come to the pool," she lamented. "She didn't feel well, and I made her come because I thought she would feel better once we got there," the mom repeated again and again.

We talked for several minutes, and then the doctors came out and informed her that they were not able to save her little girl. She immediately collapsed into my arms in tears. I held her up, and just let her cry. I had never met her, and she didn't know the man behind the uniform she was crying on, but it didn't matter. There was no one else with her in the ER.

After a few minutes, the doctors told her that she could go in to see her daughter. She immediately looked up at me and asked if I would go in with her. This is a question that has only one correct answer, so we went in to see her daughter together.

Nothing prepares you for what happens to you when you see a seven-year-old girl lying on a hospital bed with an intubation tube coming out of her mouth that is not connected to anything. I don't know why that detail is what sticks out to me. Perhaps it is because I have built a career on noticing the things that don't *fit*. I had seen breathing tubes before, but they had always been connected to a ventilator of some sort. With nothing attached to it, it was painfully clear that this little girl was no longer breathing.

I stood by the closed curtain and watched the mom apologize to her daughter for making her go to the pool. She stroked her hair and sang *You Are My Sunshine* through her tears. I didn't belong in this room, but I stayed.

I stayed because in the few minutes we spoke outside this room, we had established rapport.

I stayed because I am a dad of two daughters; I just happen to wear a police uniform for a living.

I stayed because there was NO one else with this woman who was experiencing a level of pain that I couldn't begin to fathom.

I stayed and tried desperately not to cry myself.

Eventually, family members arrived at the hospital. I gave the mom my card and told her to let me know if I could do anything to help. I also told her that I would be praying for her and her family. Sometimes, the uniform can't hide the heart.

A few days later, I was scheduled to speak at an event an hour away. The visitation for this little girl would be happening in the same city right after my speaking engagement. Since I don't believe in coincidence, I told my wife that I was going to stop in to pay my respects. She asked to come along because I had been talking about this tragedy with her for the last few days. It really hit home for both of us.

I wasn't sure the mom would recognize me out of uniform, but as soon as I walked through the door, she ran up and gave me a big hug. She couldn't wait to share with me that the autopsy revealed a massive heart issue that had previously gone undetected. Her daughter did not drown. Her heart just stopped working.

Now she knew why her daughter didn't feel good that morning. I reminded her that a trauma nurse who happened to be at the pool that day had immediately jumped in and started CPR on her little girl. An ambulance was there within minutes, and the hospital had been less than a mile away. By taking her to the pool that day, this mom hadn't caused her daughter to drown. She had actually put her girl in the best position to survive the heart attack that no one knew was coming.

Before we left the visitation, this woman shared with my wife that she believed that God had brought me to that hospital to be with her and how grateful she was for that. We all exchanged hugs and parted ways.

That day at the hospital is on my shortlist of worst days at work. But I know it was *the* worst day in this mom's life.

Rapport can be built VERY quickly in highly emotional environments. Sometimes, that puts you in the middle of someone else's pain, and sharing it can be a heavy burden. But by helping, you can ease suffering and make the world a slightly better place. One moment at a time.

I pray that you don't have to deal with something this tragic, but it doesn't take a trauma as serious as this one for rapport to be built quickly.

When a customer calls with an issue, do you simply see them as a problem to solve—another unexpected task on your To-Do list? Or do you spend a few extra minutes listening as they vent their frustration so you can better understand where they are coming from?

Either way, you provide customer service. Only one will build rapport.

SLOW & STEADY: LITTLE DEPOSITS OVER TIME

The other way to build rapport is with consistency over time. The people you lead at work will learn to trust you or hide from you by the little ways you show up every day.

When your team member walks in frazzled and late, do you reprimand them first? Or send them a webinar on time management? Or do you stop by their desk and kindly ask what held them up? They may need a louder alarm or a little less nightlife. But what if they were late because they had spent the night in the emergency room learning that a loved one has cancer?

We all want to do business with people who understand our frustrations and make it their job to help AFTER they have taken the time to listen.

I said almost nothing that day in the emergency room because there was really nothing to say.

Was it convenient? Not really.

Was it comfortable? Definitely not.

But did it make a difference? Absolutely! In both the mom's life and mine.

I built rapport that day by showing up and being present. I did not have to talk. I just had to listen. I encourage you to do the same.

As a hostage negotiator, a husband, and a dad, I can assure you … listening is EVERYTHING!

Chapter 6:

LISTENING

've heard it said that listening has become so rare today that it's like having a superpower. Sad. But true.

One could make a lot of arguments as to why listening seems increasingly scarce. I mean, our world is noisier than ever. As I write this chapter, I am sitting in a coffee shop ... my go-to writing place (because extrovert). And as I type there is music playing and several conversations happening around me (they all are boring though, so I'm making good progress). Orders are being placed at one end of the counter, and names are yelled out at the other end. Not to mention the traffic noise right outside the window and the occasional screech of tires as another college student zips into traffic on their rented electric scooter. To an auditory learner like me, sometimes it becomes too much. I like the bustle, but if the conversations around me were more inter-esting, or if I knew the song that was playing, I would not be able to write. I get WAY involved in conversations that I'm not a part of, and I REALLY have to concentrate to avoid singing along with songs I know in public. I'm a listener. So on days when distractions are high, my AirPods Pro save the day. The noise cancellation is EVERYTHING.

If listening is a Superpower, I'm in! As a child of the '80s, I grew up watching Superman, Wonder Woman, Batman, and a lot of other Super Friends. I even had a sweet pair of Aquaman Underoos when I was little. It's a shame those went away, but probably no one wants to see me in Underoos today. However, my extensive knowledge of '80s superheroes has taught me that having a superpower is Super Cool! The Super Friends helped a LOT of people in every episode.

Let's not sit here lamenting the fact that listening has gone the way of Underoos, and let's start talking about how much we would stand out if we developed the superpower of listening. Who could we help? How could we serve? How much money could we make?

At the police department, when we were looking to add a hostage negotiator to our team, we would start by posting the position internally. We were usually surprised by who applied. More times than not, it was the *talkers* of the agency that would be the first to throw their name in the hat. To be fair, there is some talking involved in being a good negotiator. However, the BEST negotiators are amazing listeners. The attitude that says, "I'm going to talk you into doing what I need you to do," is a fallacy believed by many. I can usually get people to do what I want them to do. But I don't talk them into it. I LISTEN them into it.

What do they want?

What do they need?

How can I help them?

What drives them?

What do they value?

What upsets them?

Trust me when I tell you, the more of these I could figure out, the more likely I could get you to do what I wanted. Does that sound like manipulation? Maybe. But it's not. Look at the questions again. They aren't about me. ALL of them are about the person I am speaking with. The only one who can truly answer those questions is the person I am talking to.

As a negotiator, I want a win, win, win situation. The person in crisis wins because they don't get hurt, and we can get them help once they come out. I win because I did my job. The other officers involved win because, partly through my actions, they get to go home to their loved ones in the same shape they left in that day.

In the business world, we are really good at SAYING things like "the customer comes first" or "our people matter," but I have a hard time feeling like I *come first,* or that I *matter,* if you are not listening to me! And please don't patronize me with surveys and annual reviews if you are not going to listen and implement changes when I share my frustrations or needs. We've got to care about more than our sale. We've got to slow down and listen so that everybody can win.

If listening is a superpower, that means you're born with it, right? Well, some people are better listeners from an early age, but I have never met someone who cannot be trained to listen better! So, don't just shrug your shoulders lamenting the fact that you're *not a good listener* and go back to your frustrating, no-friend existence. Listening is a skill that can be taught, and I'm going to show you how you can develop your own listening superpower.

But, as always, there's a catch. This is not some magic pill or quick fix. Like any skill, it takes work. You gotta WANT it. Then you gotta do the WORK! Ready? Let's go!

ACTIVE LISTENING

Most of you have heard the term *active listening* before, but you may not fully understand it. There's a good chance you weren't REALLY listening when it was explained. Therein lies the rub. Not listening to an explanation of active listening is too deliciously ironic to ignore!

Are you ready for what you missed? Get your notebook, because you're gonna want to write this down. Active Listening is being actively involved in listening to someone. Easy, right? If it were easy, my friend, everyone would be doing it. What are some hacks to stay actively involved in listening to someone? I'm so glad you asked.

1. Eye Contact

If you are face-to-face with someone (and in our post-pandemic world that could be on a video call), the first step is to make eye contact. Seriously. Like, turn your face, preferably your whole body, toward them and look them in the eyes.

Early on in my law enforcement career, there was a Lieutenant who was not my direct supervisor, but I would sometimes have a question that they were uniquely equipped to answer. I would walk down the hall to their office to ask my question on more than one occasion. Each time, I would stand at the open office door watching them type away on their computer. If they didn't look up, I would do that awkward knock on the door-frame with my knuckle while saying, "Knock, knock." I knew they saw me; they just didn't look up from their computer.

EVERY TIME, they would raise an eyebrow without looking away from their screen, and while still typing would say, "How can I help you?"

"I have a question," I would say.

While still typing, they would tell me to ask away.

I would spell out my whole situation.

When I was done, they would finally stop typing, look at me with a confused expression, and say, "Wait, what?"

I kid you not. EVERY time.

I would be forced to run through the whole thing again now that they were actually listening. It REALLY aggravated me. But I was the lower ranking officer, so I ran through everything twice. EVERY time.

You're not listening if you're not looking.

Here's your first hack: You're not listening if you're not looking. Our ears face forward for a reason. We need to be looking at what we're listening to. It's implicit in the original design of our face!

2. Minimal Encouragers

Now that our eyes are involved, the next step in active listening is to give *minimal encouragers (a term from the psychology/counseling world)*. This involves smiling, nodding, saying things like "okay," "I see," "go on," etc. Basically, it's communicating verbally and non-verbally that we would like them to continue talking because we are tracking along with the conversation.

The best illustration I can give of this happened early on in my speaking career. I was asked to speak for twenty minutes at a fundraising dinner for an inner-city charity. When my wife and I arrived, we were the only white people in the place … which didn't bother us at all. When my turn to speak came, I stepped up to the podium. I was about five sentences in when the first "Amen" came back from the audience. My wife said later that my whole countenance changed, and she knew that I was going to go longer than twenty minutes. FORTY minutes later, I was finished, and no one was upset—except for maybe my wife. You see, when they started giving minimal encouragers, it motivated me to keep talking and go off script based on what they responded to.

I have been blessed several times to attend churches where the congregations were predominantly Black. From those experiences, I have observed that those services are a CONVERSATION. There is a give and take between the pastor and the congregation. The church I grew up in was NOT a conversation. The sermon was a monologue with a precise stopping point, and we got out at the same exact minute every week. When I have had the opportunity to attend a predominantly Black church, the sermon has been a dialogue; it was done when the conversation was finished. And NOBODY knew exactly when that would be. It was an art … not a science.

When you are speaking with an employee or a client, PLEASE do not let the clock rule this interaction. Be done when the conversation is concluded. And the more minimal encouragers you use, the more they are going to talk. The more they talk, the more they will connect with you. Feeling *heard* is one of the things employees and clients need MOST.

3. Paraphrasing

Often, we make listening about ourselves. We hear the words, but inside we're busy planning our own response. When you make it your goal to be curious and take the time to check that you're on the same page, it tells the speaker you care enough about them to understand their needs—not just your own agenda. And that begins to build trust.

By simply repeating back to someone what they said, or what you *heard them say*, you move into advanced level active listening. Paraphrasing shows you are paying attention and communicates value to the person you are speaking with.

Paraphrasing also allows the speaker to clarify if what they SAID matches up with what they MEANT. I can't tell you the times that I have paraphrased, in a sentence, what someone took two to three paragraphs to say, and then they responded with, "That's not really the issue," or, "That's not what I meant to say." Active listening, especially through effective paraphrasing, helps the person talking process how their message is being received. Now they have the opportunity to try again and express what they mean in different words.

Once again, effective communication is a dialogue, not a monologue … making it more of an art than a science.

4. Emotional Labeling

If paraphrasing is *advanced* level, emotional labeling is *Jedi Mind Trick* stuff! This one is HUGE, but it can be dangerous. Remember the emotion vs. logic/reason teeter-totter that we discussed previously? If used correctly, this technique can help balance that teeter-totter.

First, let's unpack the *why,* because like anything, the why drives the how.

The why drives the how.

Emotional labeling is based on brain science. A team of researchers set out to see what happens in the brain when we put feelings into words. The researchers put participants under functional MRI scans and showed them pictures designed to elicit some type of emotion (fear, anger, sadness, etc.). When the participant saw an image, their amygdala lit up.

The amygdala is commonly called the lizard brain. It is a reactionary part of the brain in charge of our flight, fight, or freeze response—it is what told my daughter to hold so tightly to the tree when her kayak overturned. It is the most primitive part of our brain—responsible for survival—but no *thoughts* come from this area. So things in the amygdala need *processing*.

The researchers found that not only did the amygdala light up on the MRI when a participant viewed an image, it stayed that way. At this point, the researchers asked the participants to tell them what they were feeling. As soon as a participant named their feeling, the amygdala light turned off. This is HUGE. It means that by labeling the emotion elicited by an image, they moved the feeling into the rational part of the brain, thus deactivating the flight/fight/freeze response.

When we help someone label their emotions, we help move them from the primitive part of their brain to the rational part of their brain—from reacting for survival to thinking and responding. When people label their feelings, they balance their teeter-totter.

How do we do this in real life? It's simple, but not often easy. One wrong step and ... here, let me show you.

As a negotiator, I would often combine this skill with paraphrasing and say things like, "It sounds like that made you angry," or, "You sound frustrated by that."

Please notice the nuance here. I make a concerted effort to express the emotion by clarifying what I *think* I heard, and NOT by telling them how they are feeling. If you want to make someone angry, TELL them how they should feel about something!

When I say, "You sound like you are angry," it gives them an out if I am wrong.

They may come back with, "I am not angry, I'm just frustrated!"

BINGO! They just labeled their emotion, and we deactivated the lizard brain. What they were feeling and reacting to on a primal level has now been moved to the rational part of the brain, and we have started balancing the teeter-totter once again.

5. Open-Ended Questions

Have you ever gotten frustrated because the person you are talking with is giving you one-word answers and not doing their part to carry the conversation?

All the parents of teenagers just said, "Only EVERY day!" I get it. There were days my dog was better at conversations than my teenage daughters were. But before we get too comfortable in our rocking chairs bemoaning *kids these days*, I would submit the problem lies more with our questions than their (lack of) response.

You see when I ask my daughters how school was, their standard response is "Fine." When I get frustrated and push with a follow-up question like, "Well, did you have a good day or a bad day?" they would answer with, "It was good."

My public-school math tells me the second response was 3X as good as the response to the first question. But this isn't a math problem. This is SUPPOSED to be a conversation. I have allowed them to respond the way they did because of the crappy questions I asked.

What if I replace "How was school?" with "What was the BEST thing that happened today?" or "What surprising thing happened today?" Those are questions that cannot be answered with "Fine." They require more thought.

If you are getting unhelpful responses from the person you are speaking with, don't get frustrated. Ask better questions!

One of my favorite follow-up questions is, "Why?" If I get a one-word response to one of my accidental *crappy* questions, I can almost always ask why.

For example, if I ask someone, "How's your day going?" and they answer with, "Good" (one-word, ambiguous answer), I can fire back with "Why is that? What makes it good?" With that follow-up question, I have kicked them into a higher level of thinking.

When we use open-ended questions and engage in attentively listening to the answers, we can unlock the key to truly helping our clients, our colleagues, and even stubborn teenagers. We will learn what they want or need, what drives them, what they value—answers to all the questions I listed at the beginning of this chapter—the answers we need to best serve them.

6. Disclosing Similar Experiences

This is last on the list for a reason. You have to EARN this one. Nobody cares about your experiences until they feel like you care about them.

Oftentimes, we move to the solution too early. To be fair, there's a good chance they came to us for a solution, but if we do not engage them in a good conversation first, we may try to *solve* the wrong problem. Or just as dangerous, if you try to spit out a solution too soon—because you are busy—they will feel like you don't care about them. Talk about a rapport killer!

But when you have engaged a team member in a conversation by using minimal encouragers, asking open-ended questions, paraphrasing back to them what they were saying, and helping them label emotions, they will give you the latitude to share some potential solutions to their problems.

When you have built rapport, they will be happy to listen because you listened to them.

Keep in mind that these six skills are NOT how things are done today. Listening is more challenging than ever. Thankfully, listening is a skill that can be learned. However, it must be practiced to increase proficiency. The good news is, people tend to do business with people they like, know, and trust. And any effort to truly listen to someone is the BEST way to get there.

Amidst all the listening, you will occasionally be expected to respond. When you do, make every effort to balance clarity and kindness. These are the strategies we are going to implement next.

Chapter 7:

KINDNESS & CLARITY

have made a living from my words. As a police officer for 20 years, I talked my way out of MANY a fight. As a hostage negotiator, I talked people into peacefully surrendering and saved lives with my words. As a public information officer, I kept the public informed, calmed their fears, and helped build a positive relationship between our police department and the community we served. As a D.A.R.E. Officer, I brought my words into the classroom every week and taught fifth and seventh graders how to make better decisions. Some students took those words to heart, and some kids had to find out the negative consequences on their own—regardless of what I said. I understand, better than most people, the absolute POWER of our words.

WORDS THAT SHAPE US

If I ever had any doubt about this power, all I needed to do was look to my friend Ricky. Ricky was a fourth grader when I first met him. I was working as a D.A.R.E. officer at the time. This was one of my favorite jobs as a police officer because it focused on prevention instead of cleanup. Again, no one calls the police when they are having a good day. We are always there right AFTER the tragedy. Being a D.A.R.E. officer was my chance to prevent tragedy through education and relationship building. If I taught my lessons well, my students saw behind the badge and got a glimpse of my heart. When they felt like I cared, they would listen to what I had to say.

When you run your organization with clear communication that comes from your heart, you will prevent many disasters, and your team members will love coming to work.

Ricky was kind of a difficult story, though. You see, while I taught D.A.R.E. to fifth and seventh graders, I also interacted with the other students in each school. I got to know Ricky mainly because he was usually waiting outside the principal's office when I arrived at the school. I always arrived early—I liked to make sure I was set up and ready to teach before the students walked into class. I wanted to greet the students as they came in, instead of scrambling to set up while they awkwardly waited for me to be ready. Sometimes it's the little things that make the biggest impact on building rapport.

On one particular day, Ricky was sitting in his usual chair waiting to be seen by the principal. I could tell he was not happy, and I had some time before I had to teach, so I sat down next to him. Apparently, when you are sitting outside the principal's office waiting to hear what your punishment was going to be this time, the LAST thing you want to see is a uniformed police officer sit down in the chair next to yours. I often forgot

I was wearing a uniform in those days. When you wear something 40 hours a week for so long, you forget that your uniform evokes different emotions in different people. To me, it was just some uncomfortable thing that I had to wear—trying not to sweat under the layers of blue polyester in the humid Kentucky spring. But to someone in the general public, the handgun that was ever-present on my hip was like flashing lights. I could watch their eyes dart back and forth from my hip to my face as I walked up.

When I sat next to Ricky that day, he turned away from me. Undeterred, I asked him what was going on.

"Nothing," he mumbled and continued to look down and away from me.

Unbeknownst to Ricky, I was raising two daughters, and I was used to the *nothing* response. Remember what we discussed earlier? When you don't get the answer you can work with, ask a better question.

Ricky didn't know that my girls had taught me that behind every "nothing" there lives a "something" just waiting to be discovered. He wanted me to go away. He obviously didn't know how annoyingly persistent I can be. And so, much to Ricky's disappointment, I got comfortable and prepared myself to not accept "nothing" as an answer.

Behind every "nothing" there lives a "something" just waiting to be discovered.

With his one-word response to my question, he had thrown down the gauntlet, and I picked it up and girded myself for the battle. I mean, he was like nine years old, how hard could this be? This poor kid didn't stand a chance. He had no CLUE what a highly-trained communicator I was. Challenge accepted!

Little did I know at the time, but neither one of us would leave this battle as *winners*.

Undeterred by his "Nothing" response to my initial question, I came up with what I thought was a better question. "What's going on today?" I asked, trying to lighten the somber mood.

"Nothing," said Ricky.

Man, this kid was GOOD! Still addressing the back of his head, I told him, "If nothing was going on, you wouldn't be sitting up here. So, what brings you to the principal's office?"

"I didn't DO anything! This is stupid!" he responded.

Victory! We were making progress. That answer had WAY more words in it than his first two answers combined! At this point, the school receptionist, who apparently had been eaves-dropping on our conversation (sidebar, the school reception-ist/secretary knows EVERYTHING that goes on in a school), chimed in from across the office.

"He's up here for head-butting the assistant principal and blacking her eyes," she said.

Point of note: if you WANT to go to the principal's office, head butting the assistant principal is a pretty good way to guar-antee a trip!

Ricky still wasn't looking at me, and now I understood why. He probably thought I was there to arrest him. To be fair, assaulting a school employee is a felony offense in Kentucky. However, when dealing with someone so young, an arrest is not always the best way to handle it. Criminally charging someone so young is rare, thankfully. So I changed tactics.

"Ricky, I'm not here to arrest you. I'm here to teach some fifth graders. Lucky for you, I had some time to kill, so I sat down with you just to talk."

"I didn't even do anything," Ricky said. "That b**ch wouldn't let go of me."

I'd like to tell you that this kind of language from someone so young was surprising, but my wife has been an elementary school teacher for over 20 years, and she has been cussed out by kindergartners. So I knew that word wasn't the worst that Ricky was capable of, and I chose to ignore it. He was speaking in complete sentences now. No need to shut him down over his poor choice of words.

How often do we shut down conversations because of our perceived offense? How often do we get distracted by the trees and never make it deep into the forest? Once someone is talking, I find it's best to allow them to say things the way they need to say them … not the way I would like to hear them.

Once someone is talking, I find it's best to allow them to say things the way they need to say them … not the way I would like to hear them.

Knowing a little of Ricky's history allowed me to ignore his disrespectful tone for a minute to try to drill down to the heart of the matter. I asked him to look at me. When he refused, I told him I wasn't going anywhere until he looked at me.

I guess he really wanted me to leave because he turned his face toward me with the most hateful look you can imagine. I looked right into his belligerent little face, and with as much compassion as I could muster, I said, "Ricky, you are a good kid."

He rolled his eyes and looked away again. I reminded him that the longer he looked away from me, the longer I would sit right next to him. He looked back at me, and this time he held my gaze.

"You didn't let me finish, Ricky. You are a good kid who makes poor choices. If we could teach you to make better choices, you would spend less time in trouble and more time with your friends in class."

He was still scowling at me, but I felt like he was finally listening, so I repeated myself, "You are a good kid, Ricky."

When I said that, his eyes filled with tears; he quickly looked away from me. Between sniffles, Ricky said something that I will never forget.

Almost to himself, he said, "No I'm not. I'm not a good kid. If you don't believe me, just ask my mom. She'll tell you. I'm not a good kid."

There you have it, folks! The reason Ricky was in the principal's office—words had been spoken to him that he believed.

"Sticks and stones may break my bones, but words will never hurt me," was the line we were taught as kids. I'd like to find whoever coined that phrase and punch them square in the face. I mean, seriously? Have you ever found that to be true? I've never really been hurt by sticks and stones. Unless you count that time that I jumped into a bush as a kid and one of the branches pierced my calf (I still have a pretty cool scar). Other than that, sticks and stones have never really harmed me. But words? Those can HURT.

I believe, with everything in me, that Ricky was sitting outside that principal's office because he BELIEVED that he was a bad kid. Why would he believe it? For the same reason that I believed in Santa Claus at his age ... because the people I loved the most in this world told me so.

Psychologists call it a "self-fulfilling prophecy." I'm not a psychologist, and I didn't even stay at a Holiday Inn Express last night, so I had to look that one up to make sure I was using it correctly. According to Psychology Today, "A self-fulfilling prophecy is a belief that comes true because we are acting as if it is already true."

I'm afraid that Ricky was doing *bad kid* things because the person in his life that he loved the most had convinced him that he was a bad kid. He was acting the part. He was fulfilling what he believed, and he believed it because he was told it. Repeatedly. Instead of telling Ricky that he was a good kid, the person who was supposed to love him the most in this world told him the exact opposite. He heard it. He believed it. He became it.

WHAT STORY ARE YOU TELLING?

Sticks and stones, indeed. Words not only hurt, but they have the power to shape what we believe about ourselves. Once we believe those words, we will often become those words. This isn't just true for nine-year-old boys.

What story are we telling our team members?

What story are we inviting our customers into?

What do they believe to be true about us?

What do they believe to be true about themselves when they interact with us?

Our team members and our customers don't just want an organization to interact with. They want to be a part of a story. They want to know they matter—that you see them and believe they have the ability to overcome obstacles and make a difference. If you have not read *Building a StoryBrand* by Donald Miller, you should! No one understands the power of story better than Don. While he applies the idea to marketing and building a brand with loyal customers, the same principles apply to building a dedicated team, a positive company culture, an organization of committed donors, or a strong family.

We are storytellers, my friends. Our words shape others for good or bad. We should be using our words to invite people into an identity that will make them, and this world, better!

I don't know what Ricky is doing today. I hope someone started speaking a better story to him. I hope someone showed him that he had the power to choose his own story.

We should be using our words to invite people into an identity that will make them, and this world, better!

You have Rickys working on your team or interacting with your organization. Invest in them. Invite them into a better story.

NEVER WILL I EVER

Do you have a list of *I Won't Say That* words or phrases? You know, the ones that your boss, a teacher, or a middle school bully said to you that hurt? You may not have labeled it, but I'll bet you do. What if you made a *Words To Say* list instead?

What can you say to build people up?

How can you recognize key employees or customers?

What can you do to invite them into the story?

If we want to write a better story, we have to practice using better words. Tuck the list in your desk drawer and pull it out every Monday morning. Or take a quick look at it right before your meeting with that difficult team member. Or before your teenager rolls in past curfew. Choose your words wisely because they have immense power. And when you use them, make sure they are clear and kind.

You don't need to show up to every argument you're invited to. When someone blasts your organization on social media, the wise organization does not fire back. The most successful organizations say something like, "We are so sorry to hear that we did not live up to your expectations. We would love to speak with you about how we can do better next time. Is there a time we can connect on a brief phone call?" With a statement like that, you have shown the world (because this comment happened on the WORLD wide web) that you are willing to address their complaint, but you have moved it to a less public, more personal medium.

If you ignore their complaint, you come off as uncaring and cold. By asking them to move the discussion off-line, you show the watching world that you care. That is how you win. Show me that you care, and I will extend you a lot of grace.

CLARITY WINS

When you engage, lead with your heart, and be as clear as you can. Dave Ramsey has a quote that I often think about when I'm getting ready to have a difficult or sensitive conversation, "To be unclear is to be unkind." I TRULY want to be kind to everyone. That is a rule I have always lived by. Rest assured, I can KINDLY take you to the ground if I need to protect you, me, or those around us. *Kind* is a worthy goal. But we will not reach kind without being clear.

If the person you are speaking with is an employee, setting CLEAR expectations for their success is kind. Holding them accountable when they do not reach those expectations is the kindest thing we can do. If we desire to watch them succeed (and by extension, our organization), being clear with them is the best way to help them accomplish it.

If the person you are speaking with is a customer or client, being clear is even more important. If you cannot meet their deadline, let them know as soon as you can. If they choose to take their business elsewhere because of this, that is up to them. If you are honest with them from the beginning and set clear expectations, you can lessen this risk. But if you are NOT clear with them, or worse yet, do NOT communicate difficulties with them, and set their timeline back unexpectedly, I can pretty much guarantee they will find someone else to do the work in the future. Communicate, communicate, communicate … as CLEARLY as you can. It's the kindest way to do business.

As a negotiator, I had to learn to be VERY clear with the people I spoke with. This was difficult in the beginning. I feared that I would *plant* ideas in their mind. But the research doesn't bear this out. For example, if I was talking with someone who I thought might be suicidal, my instincts told me to avoid that topic. If I had concerns, I might ask something like, "Are you thinking about hurting yourself?" Do you see the ambiguity there? The BEST question I could have asked is, "Are you thinking about killing yourself?" The first question FEELS nicer, but it is not clear. If I was planning on killing myself, I would do it in a way that wouldn't *hurt*. So by asking if I was thinking about *hurting* myself, I could honestly answer, "No." By asking if I was thinking about killing myself, you make it more likely that I will give a clearer answer. And you will not *plant the idea*. If I was not planning on killing myself, I wouldn't start making a plan simply because you brought it up. If I was planning on killing myself, you asking directly about that greatly REDUCES the chance that I will actually do it. Do you see the difference?

You have nothing to lose by asking and everything to gain. Clarity wins. Every. Time!

Now that we've discovered that silence without rapport is NOT our friend, and we understand how to get past the barriers to effective communication, it's time to start having these important conversations. How best should we do this? I'm glad you asked. We're going to spend the next few chapters unpacking some of the more popular ways that people are communicating, and some of the pros and cons of each method.

Welcome to Training Phase Three.

TRAINING PHASE 3

The Tactics

Chapter 8:
FACE-TO-FACE

I believe, with everything in me, that if you are going to have an important conversation with someone, face-to-face is the BEST way to have it. I wish I could convince my 17-year-old of this fact. She wants to do EVERYTHING over text, and I'm just the *Old Man* who doesn't understand how people communicate today. There may be some truth to that. However, I DO know how the most SUCCESSFUL people communicate.

Successful people take care of business face-to-face whenever possible. They know that...

- The key to clarity is not just what you say, but how you say it.
- People feel seen and heard when they connect with other people.
- There's no better way to build rapport than through shared experience.

You have to ask yourself, "Do I want to do what MOST people are doing, or do I want to be successful?"

THE KEY TO CLARITY

Think about what we learned earlier. If 93% of our message is in our tone and nonverbal cues, the best way to get 100% of the message through is to be face-to-face with someone. Because here is what I know—if the words spoken do not match the nonverbal cues, the TRUTH is often in the nonverbal. We can fake our words a lot easier than we can fake our tone and nonverbal cues.

If your *Spidey Sense* starts tingling during a conversation, it is very possible that your brain picked up on an incongruence between what they said and how they said it. Just ask a teenager to take out the trash and when you see the eyes roll with their "Fine," you'll pick up on whether this is a good attitude or not. I guarantee your customer, boss, or significant other is picking up on your true message as well. "I'll look into that," typed in an email and read with the emotions of the reader can be interpreted two very different ways. But spoken, looking eye-to-eye, it will be very clear whether you're smug and annoyed or genuinely concerned. In order for others to pick up your nonverbal cues, you have to be face-to-face.

People Need Connection

Now, in today's world, video conferences are starting to take the place of face-to-face communication. I'm not mad about that. Video is the next best thing to being face-to-face. Virtual connecting started to become VERY popular around April of 2020.

Nothing like a global lockdown to force us to find new ways to communicate. Virtual communication platforms were not new at the time. I coach clients from all over the country, so I was Zooming before Zooming was *cool*. My biggest fear at the start of the pandemic was that Zoom servers would not be able to handle the onslaught of all the Zoom Happy Hours, Zoom Game Nights, and Zoom Sex that was happening (I made that last one up, but I'm quite certain it has been done … we are a crafty people when we need to be).

The lockdowns revealed our NEED for social interaction with other people. I have worked with teenagers for 20 years. Prior to 2020, most teenagers I knew really WANTED a virtual world. They were mad when you had to *old-school* call someone on the phone to make an appointment. They didn't like interacting with people face-to-face to order food. They LOVED the self-checkout at the grocery because they could avoid the awkward small talk with the cashier.

The more virtual their world could be, the happier they thought they were. They wanted all virtual all the time. Until virtual was all they had. Until they were locked in their houses with only their annoying family. Or, worse yet, in an apartment all by themselves. Their dreams of a virtual world had come true, and after a VERY short time, that dream turned into a nightmare.

As a fairly big extrovert, the lockdowns were my worst nightmare. Don't get me wrong, I LOVE my family. When the lockdowns hit and schools went virtual, my oldest daughter came home from college for several months. My wife is an elementary school teacher, so she was teaching from home. My younger daughter was in high school at the time, so she didn't even need to get out of bed to attend school! And I will FOREVER be grateful for the time we spent watching television, playing games, working jigsaw puzzles, inventing games to compete in, texting TikToks to each other across the room, and making some pretty cool TikToks of our own. Those are memories that I will cherish forever!

The problem is, I need more social interaction than the average person. One of the ways I fulfilled this need was to take a lot of walks with my family. Now, make no mistake, these were not walks for exercise. These were social expeditions. Who in our neighborhood would be sitting on their front porch during our walk? Who would be washing their car? What other extroverts would also be out walking? If I saw you on one of our walks, you were ABSOLUTELY going to talk with me. My dog eventually gave up on the *walking* part. He would just lie down in the yard of whichever neighbor I had cornered at the time. I'm not ashamed to admit that with my office in the front of my house, I could see anyone who walked down our dead-end street and passed our house. By the time they walked back by, I would be standing outside on our porch waving like Forrest Gump on his shrimp boat when he saw Lieutenant Dan. I was eager to strike up a conversation. I was like the troll on the bridge collecting the conversation tax for using my road. I was CRAVING human interaction!

Even the introverts I know struggled during the lockdowns. After we all had spent a couple of weeks holed up with no one but the people we live with, the idea of hanging out with other people who were also locked down in their houses was AMAZ-

ING! Something, ANYTHING, to fill the hole of social inter-action in our souls. Virtual book clubs, cocktail parties, holiday dinner with the extended family, and even *Hawaiian Day* at work where you could actually show up in flip-flops and shorts with a beach for your virtual background. We got to see and talk with people who were not related to us!

As I mentioned before, I used virtual tools for meetings and presentations long before the pandemic, and I can assure you, virtual is definitely the next best thing to being in the same room. But I can also tell you it is SO far into 2nd place that it just doesn't compare.

Don't Settle for Second Place

If you hadn't eaten in a month and I gave you a cracker, that cracker would be the BEST THING EVER. You would savor it. You would lick your fingers when you were done, and you would tell everyone about the amazing cracker that you ate. Not because the cracker was special, but because you were starving when you ate it.

Virtual meetings are WAY better than not interacting with people! But once I started doing live presentations and meetings again, I realized there is no way to truly replicate the power of being in the same room with people.

Sadly, while writing this book, in another anonymous coffee shop (this book is brought to you by various coffee shops and flat whites), I overheard two women in their early twenties. One of them said, "It's such a waste for them to bring me to Florida for this all-teams meeting. I mean, why don't they just send me a Zoom link? It's EXACTLY the same thing."

"No! It's NOT!" I wanted to scream (that's frowned upon in coffee shops, by the way).

Then I realized, this is not her fault. At her age, virtual is pretty much all she's known in her professional life. She just doesn't understand the power of face-to-face because she has not experienced it.

How sad.

YOUR TICKET TO BUILDING RAPPORT

I have been blessed to experience the power of being in the same room with coworkers for YEARS. In 2019, before the pandemic caused the world to shut down, I attended conferences in Los Angeles, San Diego, and Franklin, TN. I flew to Indonesia to train business owners who were struggling to rebuild their businesses post-tsunami. I could have video-ed my way into all of those events and saved myself a LOT of time on airplanes. The reason I willingly spent so much time on planes, is because I knew the power of being in the same room. I knew I could communicate MUCH better sitting across a table with someone than I could staring at the camera on my phone.

The REAL value in conferences is not the person on the stage. It's the conversations you have in the hallways, over lunch, or sharing a drink at the end of the day. Those interactions cannot be duplicated in the virtual environment. When a virtual event is over, I close my laptop, and I return to my life. When I am there in person, I make connections and have conversations simply because I am in the room.

Nothing illustrated the power of being in the room more to me than an experience we had at a Garth Brooks concert in

2014. I have been a Garth Brooks fan for a LONG time. Like him, or hate him, if you get the chance to attend a Garth Brooks concert, you should go. Now, he does televised concerts periodically, and those are amazing. But they simply do not capture the energy of being there in person.

My wife and I first saw Garth live in 1998 when he came to Rupp Arena in Lexington, KY. That show was SO good that when he returned in 2014, we didn't even have to discuss whether or not we wanted to go. We had talked up the experience so much that my wife's parents decided to go with us to the 2014 concert. We arrived as soon as they opened the doors, which was about an hour before showtime. Now, those that know me, know I am early by nature. If we are going to meet for coffee, I will be there at least 15 minutes ahead of our scheduled time. If you show up right on time, I have to fight the urge to be mad at you for making me wait. You did nothing wrong, and yet, I feel disrespected. But I digress.

We found our seats fairly quickly. Apparently, when your seats are WAY at the top of the arena, no one else in that section arrives early. It didn't matter to me where our seats were. I was PUMPED! I had already resigned myself to watching the concert on the Jumbotrons, and I wasn't mad because I was THERE. I was IN the room for this amazing event!

While we were sitting there, a man, dressed all in black, started striding up the stairs. Now, the upper arena at Rupp is just a few degrees of incline short of needing climbing gear to get up the stairs. If you lost your balance at the top of Rupp, you would tumble a LONG way before you could stop yourself. As he was hoofing it up the stairs, the extrovert in me started cheering him on. "You're almost there. You got this. Keep going!" He laughed, and when he reached us, he sat in the row behind us to catch his breath before continuing to the spotlight a few rows above us. I started talking to him about his job. He was in charge of the sound equipment, and we talked about what it was like tearing all that stuff down and setting it all back up in a new city the next day. The logistics of this were boggling my mind. I was fascinated by the whole *road crew* life.

My mother-in-law is one of those sweet southern women who can say ANYTHING without you being offended. She's just that sweet! If she looked at you and said something like, "Well, you've been eating good haven't you, honey?" You would not be the LEAST bit offended that she just told you you're getting fat. She's the BEST! So after about fifteen minutes, she turned to my new best friend the sound guy and said, "I want to know how you get those seats way down there," and she pointed to the arena floor.

He smiled and said, "You take these tickets, and you all go sit in the second row, center stage." Then he handed us four tickets.

We went from the *nosebleed* section to the second row, just like that! We were so close that when Garth shook his water bottles, we got wet. I no longer needed to watch the Jumbotrons. That's a good thing because I could not even see them from our new seats!

That type of unforgettable experience would not happen in the world of virtual meetings and presentations. That experience ONLY happened because we had a face-to-face conversation with someone. We made the effort, we got into the room, and we engaged with someone.

I learned that day that you can't buy tickets to the first two rows of a Garth Brooks concert. Those seats are reserved for people who used to be in the *nosebleed* sections. Apparently, when someone pays thousands of dollars for front-row seats, they aren't always the best audience members. However, when *regular* folk get promoted to the best seats in the house, they do not sit down the whole show. They dance, they sing, and they celebrate with the other people who did not deserve the seats they got. That energy transfers to the stage, and the whole arena benefits. You just can't replicate that experience through a screen.

Second Is Better Than Last

In our increasingly virtual world, make every effort to get face-to-face whenever you can. Some things cannot be virtually replaced.

- A scratch and sniff sticker in the mail will never sell fresh donuts the way seeing the Hot Now sign in the window of the Krispy Kreme will as you drive by. (That's the 2nd donut reference made by this police officer for those of you keeping score).
- Team building on Zoom will never create as much trust as a hands-on experience.
- Networking with conference attendees in a virtual breakout room will never be as natural as sitting down for a drink at a hotel bar.

Assess what can and cannot be replaced and make it a priority to be in person for those activities. For other areas, remember that face-to-face allows us to get ALL of the more nuanced nonverbal communication. If you can't be in person, at least use video to be virtual.

A quick, written post on your social media channels might seem like an efficient way to get news to your customers, but a video post allows them to hear your passion and see the emotion on your face—whether it's excitement for your anniversary sale or remorse for a problem you are trying to fix. Why do you think Reels and Stories have taken over Instagram and Facebook?

A Zoom meeting allows your client to hear your voice and see your face while you advise them. It also allows you to see their response and check for understanding. When their face looks puzzled, you can stop and ask if they have any questions. When they look distracted, you can re-engage them by asking a question.

A video message sent to your employees allows them to see your eyes. It also says your message is important enough that you took the time to stop and record it. You weren't simply typing a text under the table while half-listening in the management meeting. Giving just a moment of undivided attention speaks volumes.

Whether in person or virtual, the effort you make to be face-to-face will pay dividends for you and your organization!

Knowing the power of face-to-face communication, my life would have improved IMMENSELY as a negotiator if I could have negotiated face-to-face, but that is not always possible. Since I was not interested in potentially making myself a hostage, I settled for the phone. When we can't see each other, let's at LEAST make an effort to hear the sounds of voice and tone.

Chapter 9:

PHONE

My phone is a part of me. If it is not in front of my face or in my hand, you will see the outline of it in my right front pocket. Keys go in the left pocket ... everyone knows that. My phone is almost never out of reach. Is it an issue? YES. Do I care? NO. My phone allows me to connect with the WORLD, and for an extrovert like me, that puts it on the same level as crack. I would love to be strong and tell you that I could do without it, but I don't like to lie unless I have to.

For this chapter's purposes, when we talk about the phone, we are going to be talking about *old-school* use of the phone ... as in actually having a voice-to-voice conversation with another person in real time. If you are under thirty years of age, this will seem *cute*, *antiquated*, or *retro*; whatever word you are using to describe things old people do today.

As a professional speaker and a communication consultant, I use the phone a LOT. Let's be honest. When someone is looking to hire me, they often want to know that I can string a sentence together when I am speaking. Because we have all met people who can craft a beautiful or a brutal email, and when we see them face-to-face, they can't make eye contact or put three words together at a volume that can be heard. There are some things words cannot accomplish on their own.

VOICE OVER

If you cannot get face-to-face (in person or virtually), a phone call is your next best bet. When you are talking on the phone, others will at least pick up the cues in your tone. Remember that only 7% of our message is contained in our words. When we can hear the tone, we will pick up another 38% of the message. We will miss the nonverbal cues on a phone call, but 45% is a LOT better than 7%.

When I first became a hostage negotiator in 1999, a telephone was our best way of communicating. At that time, 100% of my negotiating was done over the phone. I learned as much from their tone and what I could hear in the background as I did from their words. Thankfully, back then we did not have all of today's social media, and texting was difficult. Who had time to press the 7 button FOUR times just to get an S to show up on the flip phone screen? It was a simpler time, to be sure. Here's the rub. Communication principles don't change that much over time. When it's important, do everything you can to get as much of the message as you can the first time around.

This is a numbers game. Which tactic is going to give you the best return? Profitable businesses minimize their costs, and at the LEAST miscommunications cost us money—mixed up orders, extra shipping, fines for missed contract deadlines. At the worst, we lose employees, customers, and public trust (which DOES cost us money, for all those people offended that I talked about money first). Better communication is better business.

Basic Rule: When you cannot get face-to-face, get on the phone.

Better communication is better business.

Think about the important conversations you have had in your life. I would wager that the ones you remember stand out more because of what you FELT during the conversation than because of what was said. One of my favorite Maya Angelou quotes speaks to this. She said, "I've learned that people will forget what you said, people will forget what you did, but people will never forget how you made them feel."

I can almost guarantee that if you hear me speak live, you will FEEL something during the presentation. This is not manipulative or me playing to your emotions for the sole purpose of making you feel something. This is an effort to get you to REMEMBER the key points I am trying to convey. You see, if I can get you to attach an emotion to what you are learning, you will remember it MUCH longer than if I just regurgitated a bunch of facts during my presentations.

One of the ways that our brain identifies emotions is through tone. When tone is added to the message, our brains begin to pick up on how someone is feeling about what they are talking about. When we begin to pick up on the emotions behind the words, we begin to build rapport.

Tone often communicates sincerity.

Sincerity builds trust.

Trust increases business.

Outside of my hostage negotiation responsibilities, I can think of several important times when the telephone was my primary way of communicating. I also served as sergeant of the Community Services Division. In this role, I supervised the other D.A.R.E., safety, and school resource officers. After six years of leading these teams, my immediate supervisor retired, and my new supervisor convinced the chief that the School Resource Officers (SROs) should fall under Patrol instead of Community Services.

I was not asked for any input on this decision before it was made.

I was not consulted on the timing.

I was simply called into the chief's office and informed of the change. Effective immediately and to be announced by email. That same day.

After leading these officers for six years, the last way I wanted them to learn about this restructuring was through a mass department email. I asked if I could personally tell the SROs before the email was sent out. Command agreed to delay the email announcement for two hours.

Two hours to visit all five schools, all across town, and meet face-to-face to deliver the news? There was no way to make that happen. So I chose the next best option and called each one on the phone.

Each officer heard the news from me—personally. I could not change the decision. I couldn't give them any answers because, as I said, I was not consulted on the decision. Nor did

I agree with it. However, the one thing I could still control was my relationship with each officer I had led over the past six years.

My hope was that over the phone they could hear in my voice that I still cared about them, that I wanted what was best for their careers, and that I was still simply a phone call away if they ever needed anything. An email or text message would never have adequately conveyed all of that. I needed my tone to transmit more than my words.

I needed them to hear my heart.

TAKE TIME TO STAND OUT

Business is a competitive world. Not only do you have to stand out from organizations in your area, but every other online marketplace too. How are you going to set yourself apart? You have got to be willing to do what others are not.

How much time does it take to send a pre-written response to a job posting? About thirty seconds? If you want to attract top talent you are going to have to give them more than that.

You might not be able to personally call every job applicant, but could you call the top ten? Recruiters do not email prospects—at least not the successful ones. They get on the phone. They at least leave a personal voice message. In today's tight job market, that phone call could make the difference in your people feeling like they matter—especially if you are working with internal candidates.

As the Community Services Sergeant, part of my job was serving on interview panels. It was not uncommon to have six officers apply for one open position in the Community Services Division. Once the interviews were over, and the panel had settled on a successful candidate, I would call ALL the officers that applied to give them the results—before we posted the name for the rest of the agency.

Most of those phone calls were not good news. One person got the position; the others would be disappointed. I always made a point of calling the officers who did not get the position first, before I called the one who did. I could push through the difficult calls (it's never fun to disappoint someone) knowing there was a much more enjoyable phone call to make at the end. Yet, each applicant still deserved the respect of hearing me thank them for applying, letting them know what they could work on for next time (if they asked), and informing them on who would be filling the new position. As I mentioned before, we always had a pool of applicants wanting to work on our team. Make people matter and they will want to work for you.

I have had many impactful and helpful phone calls in my life. As a hostage negotiator, I have literally been able to save lives based on phone conversations. The phone can be POWERFUL.

Until it's not.

WITH GREAT POWER COMES GREAT RESPONSIBILITY

We can do a lot of good with our phones, but they are a double-edged sword when it comes to workplace morale and team rapport.

The biggest problem with our smartphone world is the fact that our phones are ALWAYS with us. This can blur the lines of what being *off work* looks like. With our smartphones, we can receive work-related emails, slack messages, and phone calls at all hours from anywhere. Maybe I would have enjoyed being one of those people working from a beach in the Caribbean during the pandemic? But do not forget—one of the quickest ways to undermine rapport is to not respect your team's *off* time.

If you are in a leadership position within your organization, the onus rests on you to help guard off time for your team members. Just because YOU may be working doesn't mean your team members are.

If my supervisor were to call me when I wasn't at the department, I would answer the call. I was not paid to be on call, but that never crossed my mind. When they called, I answered. As soon as I answer, I am no longer in husband or dad mode. My brain switched to "Sgt. Harvey" mode. On more than one occasion, I remember *shushing* my daughters so that I could deal with a work situation while I was supposed to be *Dad-ing*.

Sometimes, these calls were actual emergencies. Too often, they were something that could have waited until I was at work. They just "wanted to call me while they were thinking about it." They wanted to "run something by me," or "get my input." These are all euphemisms for "this could have waited," but we make it sound important to justify our call. To be honest, I've done it to officers that I have supervised.

This is a failure of leadership. A small one, but a failure, nonetheless.

Today, technology has evolved to a point where this is easily correctable. I have short-term memory issues. Not because of any kind of mental flaw ... just that I am easily distracted and not always listening as intently as I should. Every now and then, I hear people talking, I nod appropriately, and I may even say something in response ... then, I walk away, something shiny crosses my path, and I forget what they said (or the fact that I answered them). Knowing my penchant (that is a word I should use more in my life ... I like the sound of it) for forgetting, I harness technology to help me with this. Siri becomes my personal assistant. Instead of calling people after hours *before I forget*, I tell Siri, "Remind me at nine in the morning to call John about the speaking gig next month." Then, like a great personal assistant, Siri adds it to my calendar. At 8:45 the next morning, my Apple Watch will tap me on the wrist to tell me that it's almost time to call John. I didn't forget AND I didn't bother John after hours.

You can get REALLY fancy, if you want, and set location-based reminders. You can tell Siri, "When I get to the office tomorrow, remind me to call Cheryl about setting up a meeting." The next morning, when you pull into the office, your phone will remind you to call Cheryl. We no longer have an excuse to bother people after hours for non-emergency situations because we can use our technology to remind us to respect business hours.

As a bonus, when I tell Siri to remind me to do something during business hours the next day, I can return to my own after-hours activities MUCH more quickly. When I know Siri has taken care of me, I can allow myself to forget about the details. I can switch back to being husband, or dad, or beating the guys at poker night—because I shouldn't be working after hours either.

To further set the boundary line, I have set my iPhone up to stop making noise after 10:30 at night. I am a morning person, so I go to bed fairly early (I'm also kind of old, but *morning person* sounds better). If you text or DM me in the middle of the night, I will see that notification the next morning when I wake up. The only way my phone will make noise in the middle of the night is if you *old-school* call me. Because, in my experience, text messages and social media notifications are never emergencies.

Phone calls are powerful. Taking five minutes to reach out to someone voice-to-voice is an investment, but the payback in trust and rapport is worth it. Choose the right tactic. Use it at the right time. And get your message heard.

Chapter 10:

PRINT

Have you ever seen a printing press in action? I'm someone who LOVES watching things get made. I love watching shows that take me behind the scenes to see how products are made in a factory. Or how someone is building a motorcycle. I even enjoy some HGTV shows where they are renovating houses. I geek out watching people fix and build things. How do they make it look so easy? Fixing and building physical things is NOT what I'm good at. What I am good at is PAYING people to fix and build things for me. My wife, even after 25 years of marriage, still thinks that I know how to do these things. She tells me all the time, "You could probably fix that." But it's the *probably* that keeps me from attempting to fix it … especially if it involves water or electricity. If you don't contain either one of those correctly, you can make the problem MUCH worse! But I digress.

The printing press. Watching someone meticulously place each letter in the tray, set each punctuation mark, and make sure the spacing of every line is correct. It's a lost art. As I type this on my MacBook, sitting in a coffee shop, I marvel at how we take this technology for granted. Part of me wants to have the newspaper (like a real, PAPER copy) delivered to my house daily, so I can hold something in my hand that someone MADE each day. As a bonus, I wouldn't have to get my *news* from my phone or computer. Now, I know that newspapers don't use hand-set printing presses anymore, but I kinda wish they did.

You see, words are *cheap* now. They are created and sent in a matter of seconds. They don't cost NEAR the time that they used to. And we are dealing with the fallout of this every time we turn around. I can guarantee you that when every letter had to be set in a tray, by hand, the words we decided to put into print meant a whole lot more. When each copy had to be run by hand, and someone had to make sure the ink was the right viscosity (isn't that a fun word), and the paper fed correctly, and ample drying time was utilized to reduce smearing—when the process took most of the day—the value of the words increased. And when you think of all the eyes that saw those words before they were released to the public ... they had been checked and rechecked. Proofed. Thought about for days or WEEKS before they were disseminated. Words had IMMENSE value back then.

I can guarantee you that when every letter had to be set in a tray, by hand, the words we decided to put into print meant a whole lot more.

I would submit to you that they have equal value today. But the problem is, most people have forgotten this. When something can be produced and disseminated SO easily, we often don't assign a lot of value to that thing. Whatever that *thing* may be. But we cannot, as a society, allow that to happen to our words. We know they have value when we receive them. We have to recognize their value when we create them.

Putting words in print must be treated with respect—and that means we use print thoughtfully and intentionally. We must not forget how the words we type...

- are open to interpretation.
- can build up or tear down.
- become a permanent record.

OPEN TO (mis)INTERPRETATION

Putting things ONLY in print limits their impact and could change their meaning without your knowledge. I was sitting in an airport not too long ago when I overheard a conversation between three people who clearly worked for the same organization. I don't intentionally eavesdrop in public, but I am an auditory learner, and I can't help it! This is why God invented AirPods Pro ... the noise cancellation in those things is RIDICULOUS. But I did not have them in that day, so I was wrapped up in this conversation happening a few feet away. It went something like this:

> Woman 1: Did you see this email from Susan?
> Man: I did. She sounded excited.
> Woman 2: Do you think? I don't know. I mean, toward the end of the email, she said, "That's awesome." What did she mean by that?

Man: I took it to mean she was excited.

Woman 1: Now that you bring that up, Susan can be fairly sarcastic.

Woman 2: Exactly. Does she mean, "That's awesome, I'm excited," or "That's awesome, one more problem for me to deal with"?

The conversation went on like this for about 20 minutes. I wish I was kidding. Twenty minutes multiplied by three employees = one hour of productivity trying to figure out what their supervisor meant when she typed, "That's awesome."

I would LOVE to train that organization! If you think they are the exception, you are kidding yourself. There are people in your organization, right now, that are trying to figure out what you REALLY meant in your last email/memo/directive. They can't help it.

If you remember back in chapter 3, when we broke down how much of our message is in the words we use, it was only 7%. When we put something only in print, we risk leaving 93% up to interpretation.

When we put something only in print, we risk leaving 93% up to interpretation.

Does that mean we shouldn't put things in print? Absolutely not. You are reading this book right now, so there is obviously value in putting things down in writing. I'm just cautioning you about communicating ONLY in print … especially with people you don't yet have a relationship with.

The more face-to-face conversations you have had with someone, the better they are at interpreting your writing. Their brain has already picked up the nuances of how you communicate. How do you joke? What bothers you? What do you value the most? What are your pet peeves? Our brain picks up this information largely by reading tone and body language. Both of which are missing in the written word. However, if I know you well, my brain will do a surprisingly decent job at filling those things in when I am reading what you wrote.

When I read a book written by someone whose podcast I listen to, my brain will even read the book in their *voice*. It will do this because I have spent HOURS listening to them. If someone has spent hours listening to you, their brains will do the same thing, and miscommunications decrease.

BUILD UP OR TEAR DOWN

I send Google Doc evaluations after my training and speaking events. Well over 90 percent of those are positive, and they mean a LOT to me. It is nice to hear from the people that you are trying to serve that they found the time spent together useful, helpful, inspirational, etc. I also value any constructive feedback they can offer. For instance, it is SUPER helpful when they say things like, "I would have liked to hear more about _____." If enough people feel that way, I will change presentations to make sure I am providing the most value possible.

Every now and then, I will receive feedback from *Anonymous*, who's my WORST critic, by the way. One time, Anonymous reviewed one of my school assemblies. They had seen my hour-long presentation about the responsible use of technology. This assembly covered social media, cyberbullying, and sexting—three areas teens often struggle with. Anonymous accused me of being misogynistic, racist (because the pics in my presentation did not show enough people of color), and wasting time, "...time that would have been better spent in the classroom." That day, I received DOZENS of comments saying this was the BEST school assembly they had ever experienced, and the conversations that happened in the classrooms afterward were GREAT! And yet, I fretted over that one negative review. Anonymous got me again.

My friend, Jon Acuff, calls it Critic's Math. He says 1,000 positive reviews + 1 negative review = 1 negative review. Now, you are probably stronger, emotionally, than Jon Acuff and me. So I'm sure this isn't an issue for you—you pillar of self-confidence.

While you may not be filling out Google Surveys, what kind of feedback are YOU sending? How many emails do your employees get about what they need to fix or do, versus something you noticed them do well? Do your clients only receive bills from you? A thank you card can go a long way in building positive rapport.

There is POWER in our words, friends!

PRINT IS PERMANENT

I just about guarantee you that people on your team have saved things you have written to them. It may be a birthday card, a memo, or an email. They are saving it for one of two reasons: either it is something they *treasure,* or it is *ammunition* for when it's time to *take you out*. Sound extreme? What's in your desk drawers or computer files? I'll bet you have both categories equally represented.

Should we be overly concerned with what is in our team members' files? I don't think so. Using our time and energy to build a positive culture is a MUCH better use of our resources and will pay dividends for YEARS to come. However, we should understand and appreciate the power of the words that we put in writing.

All of this to say, I am not *anti-print*. But it is not as clear a communication source as we believe it to be. And with today's ease of saving digital copies of everything, I would caution you to keep that in mind before you put something in writing. How many times have we seen *leaked* emails take down executives? How many *private* text messages have been shared publicly? Oh, dear friends, we need to quit acting like there is such a thing as private conversations through print. You can label it *Internal* all you want, but that is not a magic wand. When you write it down, you are, by definition, creating a record of it.

It's there.

Forever.

If I have said it once, I have said it a hundred times, anything you say can and will be used against you in a court of law—or by a competitor.

USE PRINT FOR A PURPOSE

So, when do we use print? After all, it is still a tactic we could choose for our communication plan. Let's look at three specific ways to use print on purpose.

1. Schedule and Re-Cap

While the tone or intent of a written message may be misunderstood, dates, deadlines, and details are much more clear in writing. Print is permanent and when you're scheduling an appointment or event this is a good thing. Putting the who, when, and where clearly in writing is important. You can't expect to have a great closeout sales event if your customers can't find what day the sale is. And you want to make sure your materials are delivered to the right address on the right day. Print is the key to clarity in these types of situations.

However, as we saw in the airport discussion above, tone and intent can get lost between the written lines. This is why, when I am emailing a new or potential client, I will ask them to let me know when they have 15 minutes on their calendar so that we can have a Zoom meeting or an *old-school* phone call. Some people are reluctant to commit to a 15-minute phone call saying they "don't have the time." I would submit to you that once an email chain hits three to five replies, we have already spent more than 15 minutes. Not only will we save time, but getting face-to-face (on Zoom) or hearing each other's tone (on the phone) also helps build rapport and minimize miscommunication.

After we get off the phone, I will send them an email detailing the things we discussed. This email serves a variety of purposes:

- It allows me to paraphrase what we discussed to make sure what I heard is what they meant (active listening hack here).

- It serves as a place to document Action Steps that we need to take before we can proceed (that I can easily transfer to my calendar or task manager).
- It becomes searchable. Since phone calls aren't automatically transcribed and saved (if you are reading this at a point in the future where that is standard, this is when you shake your head and smile about how quaint things were back in 2022), the Re-Cap Email allows me to search my email to remind me about what we talked about on the last call. I will reread this right before our next conversation.

Whether it's scheduling an event or re-capping a phone call, print is a tactic to clarify and remember details.

2. Reach a Wider Audience

There are times when communicating to a wider audience at once makes sense. I am a fan of all-staff emails following a meeting, customer newsletters, website content, press releases, books (since you are holding mine, I kinda have a soft spot for books), etc. It's just imperative when you put something out in print to remember that your audience can't *hear* you.

Press releases (which we will talk about in more detail in a later chapter) are a great way to let your community know what you are working on. What initiatives are you taking that affect your local community? Are you hiring? Did your organization win any awards? These are the things that will take you all of five minutes to inform your local media about. And they

MAY turn into a story about your organization. We call that FREE advertising!

Newsletters are a way to keep your customers informed as to what you have been up to. Remember, we would not be here without customers, so treating them like team members goes a long way to reinforce the rapport that you have intentionally built with them. That being said, newsletters should not be PAGES of droning on and on. Make them quick. Make them fun. Bury *easter eggs* in them (discounts, free swag if they reply, or maybe a special offer if they post about your organization on their social media). These newsletters should inform, entertain, and reinforce rapport.

All-Staff Emails keep information flowing. Just like newsletters, these should NOT be verbose. Your team has things to do! Don't bog them down with lengthy all-staff emails. This is a GREAT place to praise employees who are KILLING it, announce promotions, or issue challenges (who doesn't like a little in-office competition). Want to gamify it? Bury a challenge in the all-staff email occasionally that promises a gift for the first person to bring you a tennis ball, or a Q-Tip, or to stand at their desk and start randomly singing a song of their choice. Be creative, have fun, and build team rapport!

I'm also a fan of ending an email with something like, "If I can clarify anything in this email, please don't hesitate to reach out."

Notice I did not say, "If you don't understand this email." If there is a potential miscommunication, own it. Apologize. And move on. If they didn't understand, it's because you didn't write it in a way they could understand.

Do everything you can to choose your words wisely before you send them out. Picture someone meticulously setting every letter, space, and punctuation mark on the printing tray as you type, and let that remind you of the great care that needs to be taken when we put things in print.

3. Keep a Written Record

There are many ways written records serve organizations internally, with supporters, and in building individual rapport.

As you can imagine, we did not negotiate with hostage takers in writing. We did, however, keep written records of all our negotiations. Because, believe it or not, the people we talked to had a bad habit of getting themselves into similar situations again. If someone is suicidal, barricades themselves in their home with family members, and police are called in, there is a good chance they will repeat that behavior if they do NOT get adequate mental help. Not only did creating written records help us assess how our team worked through the crisis, but it might also allow us to expedite the process the next time.

For your organization, after an event please make a point of writing down:

- What worked?
- What didn't?
- What is something we would change for next time?
- How can we make this better?
- Are there steps we can eliminate?

Most of us are sure we are going to remember next time. I mean, how can we POSSIBLY forget? Time has a way of causing both the good and the bad to fade in our memory. The best way to remember is to have a written record.

Updates to supporters and shareholders are another important way to use written communication. Keeping people who support your organization or invest in your business informed is critical for building and maintaining trust. Often this starts with the facts and figures of a financial report or business plan. It is the record of work accomplished and accountability for goals in progress.

If you are a non-profit or community organization, sharing how your work is impacting real people does not have to be limited to dry facts and figures. My family and I sponsor children through various ministries, and it is always nice to hear what the organization is working on, issues they are facing, and ways we can pray. Communicating the impact of your work with supporters is critical, and transparent written updates build trust and partnership.

Great organizations are also keeping written records of their employees and customers. I'm not talking about the annual review, performance improvement plans, or written warnings for questionable actions or performance. Those are important records that can protect your business from a rogue or lawsuit-happy employee. But written records are not only for tracking problems. They can also help us better serve our team members and our clients.

My older brother travels a lot for his job. He told me recently how when he checked into his preferred hotel, in a city he had never been to before, the front desk associate said, "We are so glad you are staying with us, Mr. Harvey. We know you like our chocolate chip cookies, so I set a couple behind the counter here before they were all gone. I knew you were coming, and I didn't want you to miss out."

My brother was intrigued, so he asked, "How did you know to do that?" The hotel employee smiled and said, "It's in the Preferences section of your file, sir." My brother had commented months ago, at a hotel in a different city, that he loved their cookies. Someone made a note in his *file*, and the next hotel saved him some cookies. GENIUS! Write it down.

Do the rules for *writing it down* change when the WORLD can read what we write? Saddle up, partner. We are ready to enter the *Wild West* of social media where the rules are being made up as we go, and no one has *settled* anywhere yet. We are all still *exploring*, and bandits are everywhere!

Chapter 11:

SOCIAL MEDIA

Full Disclaimer: I LOVE social media. It was made for extro-verts like me. Like, seriously, as someone who loves con-necting with people, it's the best! Add on to that the fact that I own my own company, and now, I can justify all of my social media use as *market research*, or *reaching potential custom-ers*, or *brand building*. All of those things sound WAY better than *unhealthy addiction* ... but I digress.

If your organization is not utilizing social media, you should. If you are waiting for this whole social media fad to run its course, it's not. It's here. To stay. Use it or get left behind.

As someone who has been studying social media since the days of Myspace, I have learned a thing or two along the way. I have seen trends come and go, platforms rise and fall, and people blow up their lives with their irresponsible use of social media. It's a powerful tool, but we cannot use it blindly.

LOST IN THE SEA OF SOCIAL MEDIA

When I was a police officer, I dealt with the criminal cases of bullying, harassment, threatening, and sexting that felt like an every-week occurrence. Teens were using their technology every day, but no one had sat them down and explained how these tools, if used irresponsibly, could seriously hurt their reputations or get them criminally charged.

I believe, firmly, that if we give people better information, they have the ability to make better choices. It's why I have taught responsible use of technology to hundreds of thousands of middle and high school students in assemblies across the country. Nothing hurt me more than finishing a school assembly only to have a 16-year-old girl come up to me in tears saying, "I wish someone had told me this last month. I already sent him the pics. I don't know what to do." And it was utterly tragic to sit and speak face-to-face with two different teenagers who came home to find one of their siblings had committed suicide—both due, in part, to the drama they were struggling to deal with online. It's a LOT!

That's on us, by the way. As the adults of this current generation, we handed them an iPhone or iPad at a very early age, and more or less said, "Good luck." We left them to figure this whole technology thing out on their own, and then we want to blame them for messing it up?

Think about it. What other important things in their lives have we let them just *figure out*? We taught them how to say please and thank you. We taught them how to read so they could be successful in life. We taught them to shave so they didn't cut themselves. We taught them how they should expect to be treated on a date. We spent MONTHS teaching them how to drive, so we could hopefully minimize the risk of them getting into a car wreck. Why haven't we taught them how to responsibly use their technology?

Is it because we don't fully understand social media either? Is it because we just haven't known how important it is? I don't think it has been intentional negligence, but we have been negligent, nonetheless.

As much time as I have spent studying, using, and teaching about social media, it was put into the best (but saddest) perspective for me by a conversation I had with my youngest daughter. My wife, an elementary school teacher, and I set some fairly strict boundaries on social media when our kids were younger. They were less than thrilled with this, by the way. But suffice it to say, Snapchat was one of the last social media apps we allowed them to use. I always tell parents that Snapchat is the *deep end* of the social media pool. It isn't a particularly safe place to learn how to use social media. Because it gives people the illusion that what they send can only be seen by the person they snapped and is quickly deleted, it actually encourages kids to send things on Snapchat that they never intended for the world to see. It feels safe, but it's the app I have seen teens get into the most trouble with. That's why our girls had to spend a few years safely navigating the waters of Twitter, Facebook, and Instagram before we would allow them to have a Snapchat account.

Inevitably, our fifteen-year-old daughter was one of the last in her friend group to be allowed to use Snapchat. Normally this argument has never bothered me. When one of my girls would say something like, "Ellie is allowed to _____, why can't I?" I would always say, "I'm not Ellie's dad. I don't set rules for her. I set rules for you." Ordinarily, that would be where the conversation stopped. But not on this night.

On this night, she told me that her friends made plans with each other by sending group snaps. "And," she said, "they aren't going to make plans on Snapchat and then text me to include me on those plans. So I just miss out." Begrudgingly, that made sense to me. One point scored for the teenager.

Through tears, she told me how she and all her friends wish there was no such thing as smartphones or social media. I told her that we could get her a flip phone and deactivate her social media accounts. That's when she broke my heart.

"Dad, you don't understand," she said. "We all wish it didn't exist because of all the anxiety and pressure it puts on us. But because it DOES exist, if we don't use it, we are the only ones who don't know what's going on."

What started as a fun way to catch up with old friends and share funny cat videos, has turned into a hellish game of Choose Your Own Anxiety for today's teens. Do you want the anxiety created by growing up under the spotlight of social media, or do you choose the anxiety of feeling left out of the loop?

I'm so glad I didn't have to make that choice growing up. Our daughters have told us, several times, that they are jealous of our childhoods because we just played outside. We rode our bikes on adventures, got dirty, and got in fights—but they were over quickly and we were all friends the next day. And no one felt the need to document any of it for the world to see. It WAS a simpler time, to be sure.

MYTHBUSTING SOCIAL MEDIA

What does all of this have to do with the business world? I'm so glad you asked! If you haven't been paying attention the last few years, these *kids,* who grew up figuring out technology on their own, are now working in and leading our organizations. And, sadly, too many of us haven't closed the gap with them when it comes to understanding technology. I mean, it changes every day. It's hard to teach someone something we don't understand for ourselves.

But here's the rub … not understanding social media today INCREASES the chances that it will cause you problems. So let's spend a minute talking about the three most important social media myths and the truths you can use to strategically build your business on the social media frontier.

Myth #1: Personal = Private

Some of you are so cute! Some of you genuinely believe that the little disclaimer you have on your social media bio will lessen the blowback when you say something on your *personal* account that would not be popular at work. You know, that little sentence that says something to the effect of: "This is my personal account. Views expressed here are my own and do not reflect on my employer." Seems like that should cover it, right? I mean, I'm not a lawyer, but that sounds good. And if anyone gets offended by something I put on my *personal* page, I will just remind them that we have freedom of speech in this country, and that should squelch their ignorance.

Ah, if only it were that easy. My friend, sit down for a minute. This may be hard for you to hear. That little disclaimer does absolutely NOTHING to shield you or your organization from the potential negative repercussions of what you post on your *personal* page. When you post something on the World Wide Web, there is a strong possibility that the WORLD can see it. Frankly, I don't care how *private* you think your account is. All you have to do is watch the news today, and you will consistently see stories of people who got in trouble at work for things they put on their personal social media pages. If this offends you, I'm sorry.

Truth #1: It's Not Personal, It's Business

If you think about Myth #1, it kinda makes sense. If you are doing business with someone, and you see them posting things that offend you on their personal pages, but they have never said those things to you in a *professional* capacity, it creates a disconnect in your brain. Which one is the *real* them? When we see someone acting one way at work, and another way online, which person do we believe? What else are they hiding? Can they be trusted?

When I worked at the police department, we had a five-page policy on social media. If I could boil those five pages down, it would say, "You can be punished at work for things you put on your social media pages while you are not at work." Did this bother me? No. If it did bother me, I was free to resign and go work for an agency that didn't have this policy. I liked the policy. I didn't want to worry about someone who wears the same uniform as me painting me in a bad light online. When one person looks bad, it makes us all look bad. And in the world of policing, if someone mistrusts the uniform, it increases the chances that those who wear it will get hurt.

Your organization is no different. There's a good chance that the people who work with you are connected to some of your social media accounts. It's how we communicate outside of work. We message each other. We see the pics of everyone's kids winning Best Student awards. We see it ALL. This is just as important for leaders and business owners as it is for every employee. Here's why.

As the business owner/leader, you are a direct reflection of your business. Your personal brand is indistinguishable from your business brand. In a nutshell, you ARE the business. If you, as the owner, are not acting professionally on your *personal* accounts, why would I want to give you my money? That doesn't mean we have to agree, but I do expect you to be respectful online. In today's cancel culture you need to be aware of the fact that people are watching. Play nice!

If you are not the owner or leader, please understand that you are trusted by your employer to be professional. It not only affects customer opinions of your business, but it can greatly affect employee morale as well.

Hypothetically, if I know that John, my coworker, has been posting a lot lately about how he gets so mad at *those people* and how *they* act, etc., there is a good chance that I am keeping my eye on him at work. Especially if I consider myself part of the *they* that he is always railing against. I really do not want to work with him, but I do not want to make a big deal of it. I mean, he is nice enough at work, I guess. But he is on my radar, so I watch him. And in my watching, I am distracted. Depending upon my task at work, that distraction is at the LEAST costing my employer money in lost productivity and could result in me, or someone around me, getting hurt. Things said on social media, during our *personal* time, have a way of spilling over into our *work* time.

That being said, there are a lot of people using their personal social media to build their company's reputation. When they brag about the bonus they got, the kind thing their supervisor did for them, or how much they love going to work, it can pay off for their employer. In a post-pandemic world, none of us have a line of people waiting to work for us. If your employee's friends are inquiring about jobs because your organization sounds like a good place to work, we call that a win. And it's FREE!

Myth #2: Social Media = Free Online Store

For the most part, social media is how companies are communicating with their customers today. Your organization needs to have a social media presence, and those accounts need to be monitored and managed by team members who use their personal social media accounts responsibly. If your organization's social media is well managed and moderated, customers will like and trust your company more. Customers who like and trust companies tend to stick around longer and tell their friends about how awesome those companies are!

Truth #2: Social Media Is a Rapport Building Machine

Contrary to what you might believe, most people do not go on social media hoping to buy a product or hire someone to do a service for them. Social media is where we go to engage with our *community*. Your brand is a part of that community. Don't just look to sell me something with your social media posts. Aim to educate me, engage me, or to add VALUE. All of these things will factor into my decision-making when the time comes for me to buy a product or hire someone for a service.

As we discussed earlier in this book, businesses grow at the speed of rapport. We do business with organizations and people that we know, like, and trust. Social media can help develop this rapport. And since we are aware that silence without rapport feels like we don't care, we need to not be silent when it comes to our social media accounts. If used correctly, social media can help us build trust and rapport, lessening the impact of our mistakes when they happen.

With all that in mind, PLEASE do not give the keys to your organization's social media accounts to employees who do not manage their personal accounts well. With several of the social media platforms used today, it is difficult to know which account you are using when you are creating a post. It is easy to accidentally post on the business account something that was supposed to be posted on the user's personal account. I did this once. When my oldest daughter was in high school, she played on the volleyball team. After a big win one night, I tweeted, "Congratulations to the West Jessamine High School volleyball team on a BIG win tonight!" As soon as I hit *send*, I saw that I was on the Police Department's Twitter account, not my private account. The problem is, we also have an East Jessamine volleyball team who might feel slighted by the fact that the local police department decided to laud the accomplishments of the West team and not ever mention the East team. I quickly deleted the tweet from the police department's Twitter feed and tweeted it from my personal account. No big deal. But not all tweets are as innocuous as this one.

Back in 2012, during a US Presidential Debate, KitchenAid (the kitchen appliance company) tweeted this from their corporate Twitter account:

> Obamas gma even knew it was going 2 b bad! 'She died 3 days b4 he became president'. #nbcpolitics

Now, to be fair, KitchenAid quickly deleted the tweet and issued several apologies. They handled it as well as one could expect. Their senior director, Cynthia Soledad, said one of their employees intended to tweet the comment from their personal Twitter account, but sent it from the company's account instead. I get it. Accidents happen, and KUDOS to KitchenAid for how they handled this. Yet something in that statement bothered me—what was someone who tweets like that from their personal account doing with access to the corporate account in the first place?

My issue is, if one of your employees posts inflammatory things from their personal account, PLEASE do not give them access to your company account. Or some knucklehead will be using your company's mistake 10 years later as an example in a book to warn the world.

Who DO we give the keys to our social media to? That's a great question! Here are some people to consider giving access:

1. A professional Social Media Manager whom you have already researched and screened their business AND personal accounts.

2. Members of your leadership team. You have already vetted these people, and they have a stake in the company's reputation.

3. A marketing team. However, I would strongly suggest that a supervisor review posts by entry-level team members before they are published (this includes replies to negative customer feedback). If you are not planning and scheduling your posts in advance, it is time to start.

Myth #3: Everyone Understands Social Media

Remember those school assemblies that I mentioned doing? How many of your employees have had that same kind of training? How many of them understand the "magic" behind social media? Do you?

When we say that we expect our team members to *be respectful*, do we all have the same understanding of what that means? This is about more than whether we use Slack vs. Email, or what is an acceptable signature line—those are important conversations to have—but if we are not talking about what *respectful* looks like, we cannot expect everyone to fall in line. How someone handles themselves online could directly affect their employment. This is important stuff. We need to be CLEAR.

Truth #3: Set the Expectations

An important truth that I have been teaching teenagers for over twelve years is that there is no such thing as *online privacy*. It is like a unicorn.

Let me explain. Having raised two daughters, I know a thing or two about unicorns, because when they were little, they thought unicorns were pretty cool. I've seen pictures of unicorns. I have read them stories about unicorns at bedtime, and we have watched their animated adventures on television. However, I know they are not really *a thing*. It would be MAGICAL if they existed in real life. They just don't.

Online privacy is like that unicorn. You have heard about it. You may even have been taught a few things about it that might lead you to believe it is achievable. I wish it was. It would be magical if it existed. It's just not a thing.

Anything we put on the World Wide Web (social media posts, emails, text messages, etc.) can potentially be seen by the WORLD. There is no such thing as online privacy.

If you are a leader, getting your team on the same page across generations, experience, and understanding is your job. Don't assume.

I would HIGHLY recommend that you create a social media policy for all your employees codifying what can happen if their *personal* accounts begin to cause problems at work. This will FEEL like an overstep, but remember, "To be unclear is to be unkind."

If you do not know where to start with this, ask around. There are plenty of organizations that have already adopted stellar social media policies. Gather examples, and then tailor them to fit your organization's needs.

Make sure you address specifics such as:

- Is it okay to post pictures of company work? Or can they only share official company posts?
- What is considered proprietary at work, and therefore, off-limits for photographing or posting?

- Do you allow them to talk about clients, projects, or team members directly or indirectly on their social media?
- Guidelines for abusive or harassing language and behavior toward other employees, clients, customers, or vendors.
- What types of posts could cause harm to their employment, even if they are *off* work?
- How does their social media use impact the company (for good or bad)?

Clearly spelling out the rules gives your team members the best chance at succeeding. If they do not like this policy, they are free to choose somewhere else to work. Most team members are going to appreciate knowing where the boundaries are.

Hopefully, by now, you see the merits of engaging with your customers on social media, and you respect its power. Now, have fun with it. Surprise and delight! Be unexpectedly witty (see the Transportation Safety Administration's account, @TSA, on Instagram for examples). Social media is the fast lane to building that likability and trustworthiness.

But what if you are looking for MORE ways to engage your customers and you are already KILLING it on social media? The next chapter is for you.

Chapter 12:

OTHER MEDIA

Your organization is doing good work, and the world would be a better place if you could do more of that work. The problem is that the world doesn't know about the work you are doing because you are not talking about it in the places that matter the most.

You may be OWNING the social media space, and it feels like everyone is pushing you in that direction. To be fair, I think you should ABSOLUTELY be doing the whole social media thing. I mean, I wrote a whole chapter about it. But, make no mistake, social media can be fickle. The algorithms change daily (every time I use the word algorithm, Gloria Estefan sings it in my head, "The algorithm is gonna get you…" I know that's not the actual lyric, but she sings it to me anyway). Just because you have THOUSANDS of followers on social media does not mean they all see all of your posts.

Social media platforms are BUSINESSES. They make money; they just don't make it real clear how they make this money since the platform is free to users. In a nutshell, it's a pay-to-play game. Either users pay a subscription fee, or they promise business folks like us that more people will see our posts if we pay to promote them. I'm not saying you should not pay. I am, however, telling you that if ALL you are doing is social media, there's a good chance you are not even reaching the people who follow you, let alone those folks who avoid the whole social media thing (those people are probably busy actually living life instead of posting about it).

So, how do you reach a wider audience? How do you tell more people about how you can help them? Just drop the word *social* from social media. Traditional media has been telling stories for hundreds of years. Newspapers, radio, and television are always looking for stories. We have stories. Do you see the potential synergy?

Traditional media has been telling stories for hundreds of years. Newspapers, radio, and television are always looking for stories. We have stories.

Some of the options we'll discuss will fit your organization better than others. Some media is more targeted to local audiences. If you are a realtor, doctor, or cleaning service, this is where you should focus. You want to reach your town and not necessarily readers three states away. If you are an insurance agent or the owner of a Family Fun Center, you may want to reach potential clients from across your state or region. Choose your media options appropriately.

Before you discount any of them, let's talk about the potential each opportunity has to offer.

Local News

Some of you just dug in, and you started saying things like, "I hate the media. They are SO negative. They are always trying to trap someone to make them look bad. I don't trust them at all." Sadly, the media has gotten a bad rap. I have railed against them myself. It's easy to bash the collective *media*. They are faceless. They are a machine. But your local media is NOT that.

Your local media is made up of people who live in your community. They have families. They are every bit as real and as human as you are. And here's the game changer, they are on YOUR side! They want you and your business to look good. These reporters, these people, are just as tired of the negativity as you are! They WANT to run positive stories … when there's room to cover it. Of course, there is not always room. They will not cover your story on a busy news day. If the President comes to town, a tornado hits, or some other major event bumps your story, it feels personal. It is not. What is SUPER important to us, is not always what's most important to the community.

So how do we combat this? How do we time the market? How do we force them to cover OUR story?

We don't.

There is no magic pill.

We don't control what gets covered. That is their job. Our job is to tell them what we are doing. And that happens when we send out press releases.

Did your organization win an award? Send a press release.

Did one of your team members do something cool? Send a press release.

Is there an industry conference coming to town? Send a press release.

Are you looking to hire more workers (aren't we ALL in a post-pandemic world)? Send a press release.

Launching a new product or service? Send a press release.

We don't control what gets covered.

Will your press release cause them to cover your story? Maybe not. But I can guarantee you this, if you do not tell them about the story, they will NOT cover it. They are busy. Help them out. Send them a press release that gives them the who, what, when, where, why, and how. Because here is the bottom line: If they DO cover the story … it is FREE!

Like social media, having your local media cover your organization is making deposits in the bucket of public opinion. When your community sees all the cool things you are doing, they will tell their friends about it. They will advertise your company for you because there is a certain amount of pride and ownership we feel when an organization in OUR community is doing good things. Make enough deposits in their bucket, and there will be plenty of room to withdraw a little from it when we make a mistake.

When I worked at the police department, we sent out press releases almost every week. Some of them did not make the news, and that was okay with me. Most of those releases were just to inform the public about things we were working on. They weren't always SUPER interesting, but we sent them out anyway. Sometimes it surprised me what got picked up. Some of our smaller stories BLEW up, while others that we thought were a BIG deal never saw the light of day. But here's what I knew for sure: we were supplying content and building a relationship.

I always viewed the media as coworkers. Ultimately, we have the same goal—to keep our community informed. As discussed earlier, any big or potentially controversial story will come out. If my organization is involved, I want to be the one telling the story … especially if we messed up. It is not *spin*; it is controlling the narrative. It is time to own it, apologize, and move on.

Taking the time to establish a relationship with your local media outlets will pay dividends. If a reporter knows you and your business, they will be more likely to contact you before running a story that might affect your organization, giving you the chance to tell your side of the story. When they are looking for an expert to chime in on a topic, they will go to people they know first.

To be fair, there were certainly times that I called in favors for the police department—times when I called reporters that I had worked with a lot and asked them to please run a story. But those times were rare. And they only happened because we had been in constant contact for years.

In my experience, the media appreciate the people who make their lives easier by providing a lot of their content—even if they do not always run it. It is in their best interest to maintain all the healthy relationships that they can.

We went as far as inviting one of our local television reporters to attend our Citizen's Police Academy and told her she could bring a camera with her and document the whole experience. She and her cameraman attended 12 classes where they learned all the details of law enforcement and could experience what being a police officer is like. They conducted mock traffic stops, searched buildings (armed with cap guns) for suspects, and negotiated on the phone with someone in crisis (played by yours truly) trying to work out a peaceful resolution. We even took them to our firing range and taught them how to safely fire our handguns. This station ran a series of stories on the news, and our agency got a LOT of positive feedback.

Even though that reporter has moved on to another market in Minnesota, I still consider her a friend. This is what working with the media CAN and SHOULD look like. But you will not get coverage if you do not ask for it.

I get it, your local media may not be interested in a day-in-the-life story about what your organization does, but there's a good chance they would be interested in one of these:

Celebrations: From industry awards to 25 years in business, send a press release. We've all seen the local *Teacher of the Year* highlight stories. What can you invite the community to celebrate and recognize along with you? Send the press release.

New Products: Are you launching your Kickstarter? Have you developed a new product? Send a press release (and maybe a sample, too).

Events: Non-profit organizations frequently host fundraising events, community work projects, and celebrations. Invite the media! If your business is an event sponsor, collaborate with the organization you support and make sure you're both getting the word out to local media. Send the press release.

Local Impact Stories: This might be easier for non-profits to see: the food bank served 500 meals, the kids cause handed out 200 school supply packs, the nature group built or cleared 18 miles of trails. But for-profit businesses can make a difference too. Did you create jobs? Have you hosted high school students as part of a job shadow day? Do you give a portion of your profits for senior services or youth sports? Send the press release.

Your local media probably cares more about your community's image than you give them credit for. Make it a point to build a relationship and keep them informed.

Podcasting

Podcasting is one of the biggest, and yet often overlooked, ways of communicating a message today. If you are reading this book, there is a REALLY good chance that you listen to podcasts. How do I know this? If you made it this far, you clearly value learning and/or being entertained. While you paid money for this book (thank you, by the way … raising daughters is EXPENSIVE), podcasts are FREE. You could launch a podcast this week for less than $100. USB microphones are SUPER inexpensive, editing software is often free (I use GarageBand which comes preloaded on any Apple computer), and podcast hosting services are usually under $20 a month for the basic plans. Your biggest expense will be time, and if you want to minimize that expense, there are freelance podcast editors that will take your recorded content and turn it into a podcast for you.

How do we justify the cost of adding a podcast? Is this a fad that will move on? Will we just be throwing money away? These are all valid questions. Let's unpack some of the benefits of having your own podcast.

In the United States, over 144 million people listen to podcasts. Podcast listeners spend on average six hours and 37 minutes listening to podcasts every week! What if 30 minutes of that time was spent listening to YOUR podcast?

There is not a more intimate way to get in your customers' heads, by the way. Remember what we talked about when it comes to using the phone and the power of your voice? Only 7% of our message is in our words, but 38% is in our tone and inflection in our voice. If your voice was in the ears of potential customers for 30 minutes at a time, what would that do for your relationship? What would that do for your credibility? What bridges could you build during that time? People won't watch a 30-minute YouTube video. They won't spend 30 minutes reading your company newsletter. But they WILL listen to you talk for 30 minutes while they drive, mow the lawn, or workout. How much is that type of attention worth to you?

A podcast can cast you as an industry expert. If you are consistently educating, informing, and talking about your niche on a podcast, it won't take long before you are seen as an expert. People do business with those they like, know, and trust. If you are in my ears 30 minutes at a time educating or entertaining me, it won't take long before I begin to like, know, and trust you more.

An often-overlooked benefit of having a podcast is your opportunity to network. Interviewing other people builds collaboration—your listeners' trust will grow by hearing you interact positively with guests. And when you generously share your audience, you also tap into theirs. On my podcast, *The Speaking of Harvey Podcast*, I have been blessed to conduct NUMEROUS interviews for my listeners. Guests so far include Cliff Ravenscraft, Clint Pulver (whose book *I Love It Here* is a MUST read for business leaders), Grant Baldwin, Jeff Goins, Courtney Roselle (East Region NBC *Titan Games* Champion), Sonya Jones (runner-up on *The Biggest Loser*), and MANY more. I may not have known these people before having them on my show, but I now consider them friends. I shared my platform with them and learned from them, and it only cost them about 30 minutes on Zoom.

Who could you connect with? Who would LOVE to speak to your audience? Whose audience would you love to address if you appeared as a guest on another show? How many of your customers could you have on your podcast sharing their success stories? At this point in your business, can you justify NOT having a podcast? Maybe. But if you choose not to, ask yourself who will become the industry expert in your absence?

Write a Book

Is speaking into a microphone not your jam? What if you wrote a book? What could that do for your business? What doors could that open? I have been wanting to write this book for five years.

I started it several times. What pushed me over the edge? I realized that as much as I loved speaking on stages and conducting boardroom trainings for organizations, those are hard to scale. I will ALWAYS do those things, but they take me away from my family. This book allows me to share valuable content without leaving my house. And it allows you to learn at your own pace. We both benefit.

Will this book bring me more business? I hope so! But it also makes me better at what I do. The research, the writing, the collecting stories … they will all make my in-person trainings better! What would writing a book do for you? It's something to consider.

Start Small

Maybe you do not have time, or the patience to write a book. Perhaps a podcast sounds like a big commitment. I get that. It is not for everyone. This chapter is here to push you to find YOUR thing. What is one way YOU could communicate with your employees or customers that would set you apart?

It could be as easy as capturing the power of the camera that is in your pocket or sitting next to you as you read this book. Do you want to impress your customers with $0 investment, and 30 seconds of your time? Send them a video message instead of a text. Grab your phone, hit record (raise the camera angle a little so your face magically loses 30 pounds and a few chins), and send them a personalized video. Something like, "Hey Marcus, thank you for reaching out to Speaking of Harvey (insert your organization there … unless you want to work for me … then we should talk first). I was talking to my team about the issue you are having, and we are committed to solving your problem for you! Let's schedule a time where we could jump on a 15-minute call and get more of the details so we can serve you better. I look forward to connecting!"

BOOM! Hit send.

Or, what if, instead of a boring Friday email to your team, you sent a video celebrating wins while calling out by name the people who are KILLING it?

What if you sent a personalized video to a team member who may have had a rough week? Could your words serve to build them back up? Would they hear the compassion in your tone instead of reading judgment in a text? Investing two minutes to record and send a 30-second video could make all the difference.

The possibilities are endless, and you can have a HUGE impact.

Anyone can send a boring email. Emails take longer, they feel generic most of the time, and they are the junk mail of today. But when I get a video message that uses my name, I feel seen and valued in a way that an email will never do. I can send a video MUCH faster than I can send an email. And, as we discussed earlier, the video allows my customer to see my non-verbal cues and hear my tone. They can look into my eyes, see my concern for their problems, and hear my resolve to do better.

It's personal.

It's real.

And VERY few people are doing this.

Be different.

Use the technology you already have in an unexpected way.

Surprise and delight.

Then, send me a video message telling me how well this has worked for you! My email is Scott@speakingofharvey.com. (Seriously. If Bob Goff can put his personal cell number in his books, I can at least share my email!)

I look forward to hearing from you!

Breaking the silence in today's world requires navigating the barriers to communication, putting people—and building genuine rapport—first, and choosing the best tactic to minimize miscommunication and get your message heard.

It is more of an art than a science.

There is no formula.

You will make mistakes, but you will communicate your way through those as well. Your team members and customers will see someone making an effort. They will see someone who cares enough to break the silence that is killing the situation.

It won't be easy, but it will be worth it.

Because there is a LOT at stake.

Hang with me now. It's time for The Debrief.

The Debrief

Chapter 13:

LEGACY

I t was the early morning hours (around 0715) on March 11, 2015. I was sitting in my office having just gathered my D.A.R.E. supplies as I had four classes of fifth graders waiting for me that day. When my phone rang, I was surprised to see my supervisor's number on the caller ID. I was more surprised by what he had to say, and my D.A.R.E. bag sat untouched for the next week.

As we talked in the introduction, I cannot emphasize enough the importance of training. If you apply the tactics in this book, practice them frequently, and refer back here periodically to refresh your memory, you will be able to perform when needed. And you never know when that will be, so be READY!

As mentioned, flag folding was something our Honor Guard trained seriously for. I can't tell you the number of times I left trainings with cramps in my hands due to repetitively folding a flag. Little did I know how important these training sessions would prove to be.

In May of 2013, I posted a pic of one of these trainings on Instagram. We were folding the American flag over an empty casket, and my caption read, "Honor Guard practicing for something we never want to perform." Standing at the head of the casket in the pic was Burke Rhoads, one of our Honor Guard members who had also served in the Army.

Fast forward about twenty months to that early morning call in my office.

My D.A.R.E. bag was packed beside my desk when my supervisor called. He said, "Burke's been in a wreck, and it's not good. Can you go to the hospital to help out with his family and deal with any media that shows up?" I assured him that I was on my way. I called the school where I was supposed to teach D.A.R.E. that day and told them I would be late.

My agency served a bedroom community to Lexington, Kentucky, and Burke had been transported to a hospital in the city. When I got within five miles of the hospital, rush-hour traffic slowed me to a crawl.

At this point, a Lexington officer friend of mine called me and asked, "Are you on your way to the hospital?"

"I am," I said, "but your traffic sucks, and I am at a standstill."

He said, "Turn your lights and siren on and get to the hospital NOW!"

That was all I needed to hear. I parked outside the ER within a few minutes of his call.

There were already a dozen uniformed officers from several jurisdictions lining the halls of the ER. I went back to where

Burke was, and I saw a room full of medical personnel working on him. I got out of their way and went back toward the ER entrance to look for Melissa, Burke's wife, who I knew was on her way. When she arrived, all the officers hugged her, and I took her off into a waiting room to get her away from all the attention. I tried to reassure her. We talked about how strong Burke was, how stubborn he could be, and how we were certain that he had been driving ONLY the speed limit with his hands at 10 and two because THAT's the kind of rule follower that Burke is!

I learned later that it was EXACTLY how he had been driving on his way to training that morning. The problem was it had been a foggy morning and a car turning onto the highway that Burke was traveling on didn't see him. It clipped the back bumper of his cruiser and sent him sliding sideways into oncoming traffic. An SUV hit him broadside, obliterating his passenger seat and intruding halfway into his Crown Victoria.

Melissa and I were talking when the doctor came in. He explained that they did everything they could, but Burke did not survive his injuries.

The shock was intense. Melissa had just kissed him goodbye a few hours ago, after they finished their morning coffee. How could this be happening?

I slipped away long enough to call my wife to tell her that Burke did not survive. I barely got the words out. The unspoken tension hung on the line. With my 17 years of law enforcement at the time, we were painfully aware of the fact that this call was every police spouse's worst nightmare. It wasn't me, but it could have been. We wore the same uniform. We did the same job. We were part of the same *family*. It hurt on many levels.

Sadly, when I went back into the waiting room with Melissa, it was clear that she was not going to have a lot of time to process the shock because their kids had started showing up at the hospital. Family friends had gotten all three of them out of school—the oldest was only thirteen.

I stood in the private waiting room while Melissa explained to her kids that their daddy had been in a car wreck and he had not survived. And, most difficult of all, when the doctors got Burke cleaned up, I went into the room with Melissa and the kids as they saw him for the first time since he left for training that morning. It was the worst day of my career, by far, and I cannot even begin to imagine how hard it was for Melissa and the kids.

Shortly after this, my supervisor called me aside and told me that command wanted me to serve as the Family Liaison for Burke's family. This meant that I would be helping the family with WHATEVER they needed. I would be the point of contact between the agency and the family. I would assist Melissa with the funeral arrangements. Now, I had never planned a funeral, but as an Honor Guard member, I had attended several trainings about what was needed in a situation like this. Once again, when it hits the fan, we fall back on our training. We train for the worst-case scenario and then pray to God that we never need to use it.

When it hits the fan, we fall back on our training.

Over the next several days, Melissa and I planned a funeral that would be attended by thousands of police and civilians from all over the country. We made sure that Burke received ALL the honors that were befitting a man who had protected and served his whole adult life … first in the Army, and later for the police department. I spent more time with Burke's family that week than I did with my own, and my family was perfectly fine with this. The unspoken understanding in police families is that had it been me, someone would be taking care of MY family like I was taking care of Burke's.

In addition to the Family Liaison duties, I was still our agency's public information officer. I did countless interviews telling the media all about the type of officer that Burke was, and how the community could best honor his legacy.

In May of 2016, I flew with Melissa and the kids to Washington, DC, for Police Week. Burke's name had been added to the National Law Enforcement Memorial, and it was read on the West Front Lawn of the United States Capitol in a ceremony commemorating each officer who died in the Line of Duty the previous year. My family flew separately, and our Honor Guard and Command staff drove to DC to participate in the ceremonies. While in DC, I continued to talk to any media outlet that asked for an interview because I wanted to tell Burke's story. It was the best way I could honor him.

It was a beautiful week full of tears shed, healing laughter, and conversations over drinks.

When I arrived back from DC, I turned in my Honor Guard uniform. I had been an Honor Guard member for a long time. I was three years from retiring, younger officers were waiting for someone to leave the Honor Guard so they could apply, and I couldn't bring myself to do another parade or graduation ceremony. I felt like I had fulfilled my task, so I stepped aside to make room for the next officer.

Over that year, I spent a lot of time wondering why I was asked to serve as Family Liaison. I had never done MOST of the things that a Family Liaison is supposed to do. I had never planned ceremonies for a Line of Duty death, thank God. I had basically ZERO experience. But I did have training. I had honed my ability to communicate under pressure as a hostage negotiator. I had done countless media interviews under stressful conditions. I had comforted other families when their loved ones had been killed. I led with my heart, and I didn't try to hide that.

I still didn't feel ready to do what I was asked to do. There was a moment when I wanted to tell my supervisor no. I mean, who am I to do this? The thing that felt *safe* was to politely pass on this assignment due to my perceived inadequacies. Surely, someone else could do this better than me? But, as we discussed earlier, sometimes grabbing what FEELS *safe* is the very thing that will keep us stuck in the rapids struggling to breathe.

I trusted that my supervisor saw something that I didn't, and I let go. I let go of my fears. I let go of the fact that I had never done this before, and I trusted my training. Melissa and I talked a LOT about what she and Burke wanted. And we simply did the next right thing … one step at a time.

Looking back on this experience, being asked to be the Family Liaison was the saddest honor I have ever been given. It was the worst and the best experience of my police career. I realize that it was my training and practice—training I never wanted to use—that prepared me to take on the most important task of my career. To honor a GOOD man, and to help his family in any way that I could.

I asked Melissa for permission to share Burke's story here, and she said, "That's the only way he stays alive, Scott." So I humbly share Burke's story to inspire you to be better at what you do because life is unpredictable.

There will come a day when tragedy strikes your organization. I pray that it is not a death, but it could be. And I want it to be YOU that they give the important tasks to! Why you? Because you will actively listen your way through the crisis. You will speak from the heart so that people know how much you care. You will not hide behind the perceived safety of silence, and you will use your words to begin the healing process.

You will not feel ready, but if you are tasked to do this, there will be a reason for it. Perhaps the person who will ask you to step into this important role sees something in you that you can't yet see in yourself.

If you apply the strategies and tactics talked about in this book, you will be ready. Because here's what I know: Becoming a better communicator isn't just for work. Improved communication makes you a better spouse, a better parent, a better friend, and a better coworker. I saved the work category for last on purpose.

Because here's what I know: Becoming a better communicator isn't just for work. Improved communication makes you a better spouse, a better parent, a better friend, and a better coworker.

My prayer is that no one stands up at my funeral and talks about what a good employee Scott was. I want them to tell story after story of times when I was a good husband. A good dad. A good friend. Those are the things that matter. Those are the things that transcend time.

I keep a picture of my wife and daughters on my desk, and it is one of the last slides I show in any of my presentations. Because THEY are my *why*. Those girls are why I work. Those girls are why I go to the gym. They are why I try to eat healthy (darn you peanut butter pie!). They are my *why*. The picture serves as a reminder because there are days when I don't WANT to do the things that will provide for them. There are days I don't FEEL like being nice. There are days when I don't FEEL like writing. There are days when I don't WANT to travel to train another business. But I don't rely on how I FEEL. I have been given important tasks to get done.

We can't wait until tomorrow to start making a difference. We have to do that TODAY … because that may be all we really have.

Let go of what FEELS safe. **You've been holding on to silence for too long. Let go of your fear of saying the wrong thing.** Let the current wash you downstream to a place where you can get your head above water. Get your feet under you. Look around. And begin to speak up. Because as scary as letting go seems, it's sometimes the only way to keep from drowning.

You can do this. You're ready. Those that are too scared will never let go, but that's not you.

You've trained for this.

It's LEGACY time.

Let's go!

BONUS CONTENT

Keep up your training with more FREE *Silence Kills* content.

▌'m not one to write in a book. I will highlight and underline, but I am not going to answer questions in a book. However, I DO like to push deeper into the topics that I am reading about. That is exactly why I have more FREE resources for you.

Scan this QR code or visit www.SilenceKillsBook.com to find BONUS content to help you take your communication to the next level.

I will not be checking this "homework" because I am all out of scratch-and-sniff stickers for those that do a good job. However, as with anything, you will get out what you put in. My prayer is that this book will serve as a resource for you when those difficult discussions need to happen. These resources will serve to tailor the experience more specifically to your needs.

There is no additional charge for these resources, by the way. They're my free gift to you.

Scott

ACKNOWLEDGMENTS

This is kinda crazy.

I always wanted to write a book, but I didn't think I ever would—and here we are.

This book has been released into the wild not because of any awesomeness on my part. This book exists because of the amazing team I have surrounding me.

I have to begin by thanking my beautiful wife, Greta. You believed in this book more than I did. However, you have a habit of GREATLY over-estimating what I am capable of, so it took me longer than it took you to see this book as a possibility. I love this about you, by the way. Your unwavering belief in my abilities has pushed me through more difficult situations than you can imagine. I want to believe in me the way YOU do! Thank you for loving me well and managing ALL the things while I was in the final sprints of this project! I love you, forever.

I also want to thank my daughters, Grace and Maryn. You all have allowed dad to use you as examples in COUNTLESS speeches, and now in book format. Being your dad is one of the biggest joys in my life, and I am so thankful that God gave me the two of you. You girls have taught me that girl power is a REAL thing (and one of the strongest things on the planet), that God can seemingly carbon copy your mom and I and still leave out some of the stuff that wasn't so great on the original models, and that sometimes tears are not only needed—but healthy, necessary, and cleansing. I love you girls, more than you will ever understand.

To my fellow Transformation Mastermind participants: Mark (our fearless leader), Chad, Josh (a.k.a. Matt's brother), Jon, Rich, Jim, Russ, Matt, and our honorary member Jocko. Thursday mornings are one of the best mornings because I get to start it with some of the finest gentlemen on the planet. Your fingerprints are all over this book. You allowed me to bounce ideas off you and monopolize conversations; then you offered me constructive criticism without hurting my feelings. This is a better book, and I am a better man because of our group. Thank you, gentlemen.

To Christine and David, the most steadfast members of my High Impact Communication Mastermind, your input in this book did not go unnoticed. We workshopped titles and talked about the key concepts. Your excitement about this project was a motivator for me. It is a blessing when clients become trusted advisers and friends. Thank you!

To Tara Cooper, my editor, where do I begin? This book is my content, my voice, and a look into my chaotic brain, but it is being released into the wild because of your ability to bring it out of me. You mapped out the whole process, set "due" dates (which were HUGELY helpful for the obliger in me), polished my writing until it shined, and allowed me to see the VALUE in what we were bringing into the world. My ideas ALWAYS sound great in my head, but you made them sound great on paper too! Thanks for tolerating my twenty-four-hour texting, my panic when I felt overwhelmed, and my desire to use all CAPS to show emphasis like I would when I speak on stage. I hired an editor, and I ended up with a friend. Thank you! I'll be in touch when Book Two surfaces in my brain.

Jon Acuff and I had coffee once, in 2018, for about ninety minutes, so we are pretty much BFFs! He may not know this, but it's what I tell people. I am truly thankful for Jon's books. I have read all of them, and they showed me that writing didn't have to be "stuffy" to be helpful. Jon's writing showed me that humor, which I love, not only *can* be mixed into a "business" book …but SHOULD be! Thank you, Jon, for always making time for the people coming behind you. (Side Hug)

I am also thankful for Karen Anderson at Morgan James Publishing. When I met Karen at a conference and bounced my book idea off her, her enthusiasm pushed this dream to the front of the line in my list of tasks. As a first-time author, I understand that I am a gamble for any publisher, but Karen never made me feel that way. Thank you for taking a chance on me!

Saving the best for last (because I read somewhere that the last shall be first and the first shall be last), I want to thank God for the platform He has allowed me to build. Speaking, and now writing, are my ministry, so none of this belongs to me. I am just trying my best to love God and love people as I steward this ministry. Some days, this is easier than others. On the days that I fall short, I am thankful for His grace.

"No matter who we are
No matter what we do
Every day we can choose
To say…
If You wanna steal my show
I'll sit back and watch You go
If You got something to say
Go on and take it away
Need You to steal my show
Can't wait to watch You go
So take it away"

Toby Mac, "Steal My Show"

ABOUT THE AUTHOR

Scott Harvey is a sought after speaker, coach, and business communications consultant who helps individuals and organizations communicate through any situation. Since launching Speaking of Harvey Inc. in 2010, Scott has had the opportunity to speak and train for organizations from Kentucky to Indonesia. He also hosts the Speaking of Harvey Podcast.

As a former FBI-trained hostage negotiator and public information officer, Scott knows what it means to speak up when lives are on the line. He is passionate about helping others build the skills and confidence to move off the sidelines and lead the conversation.

Scott can still be found giving his heart and wisdom to help teens navigate communicating in an online world and to prevent tragedy before it happens, something he became passionate about in his years as a D.A.R.E. officer. He lives in Central Kentucky with his beautiful wife of more than 25 years and his two daughters.

NOTES

Chapter 2: The Brain

The 7-38-55% communication rule: "Albert Mehrabian."
Management Thinkers, Business and Management Portal.
The British Library. https://bl.uk .

Chapter 3: Stress

Teeter totter of emotion in hostage negotiation: Stratton, J.G.
(1978). The Terrorist Act of Hostage-Taking: Consider-
ations for Law Enforcement. *Journal of Police Science and
Administration, Vol 6, Iss 2, pg 123-125*

Chapter 6: Listening

Eye contact: Kreysa H, Kessler L, Schweinberger SR. Direct
Speaker Gaze Promotes Trust in Truth-Ambiguous Statements. *PLoS One.* 2016 Sep 19;11(9):e0162291. doi:
10.1371/journal.pone.0162291. PMID: 27643789;
PMCID: PMC5028022.

Emotional labeling: Lieberman MD, Eisenberger NI, Crockett MJ, Tom SM, Pfeifer JH, Way BM. Putting feelings into words: affect labeling disrupts amygdala activity in response to affective stimuli. *Psychol Sci.* 2007 May;18(5):421-8. doi: 10.1111/j.1467-9280.2007.01916.x. PMID: 17576282.

Chapter 8: Face-to-Face

Importance of nonverbal signals: Creative Commons. "Nonverbal Communication: Principals and Functions of Nonverbal Communication." In *Communication In the Real World*, adapted by University of Minnesota. University of Minnesota Libraries Publishing, 2013.

A free ebook edition is available with the purchase of this book.

To claim your free ebook edition:

1. Visit MorganJamesBOGO.com
2. Sign your name CLEARLY in the space
3. Complete the form and submit a photo of the entire copyright page
4. You or your friend can download the ebook to your preferred device

Morgan James
BOGO™

A **FREE** ebook edition is available for you or a friend with the purchase of this print book.

CLEARLY SIGN YOUR NAME ABOVE

Instructions to claim your free ebook edition:
1. Visit MorganJamesBOGO.com
2. Sign your name CLEARLY in the space above
3. Complete the form and submit a photo of this entire page
4. You or your friend can download the ebook to your preferred device

Print & Digital Together Forever.

Snap a photo

Free ebook

Read anywhere